The Cambridge Introductio
Herman Melville

Despite its indifferent reception when it was first published in 1851,
Moby-Dick is now a central work in the American literary canon. This
introduction offers readings of Melville's masterpiece, but it also sets out
the key themes, contexts, and critical reception of his entire oeuvre. The
first chapters cover Melville's life and the historical and cultural contexts.
Melville's individual works each receive full attention in the third
chapter, including *Typee, Moby-Dick, Billy Budd* and the short stories.
Elsewhere in the chapter different themes in Melville are explained with
reference to several works: Melville's writing process, Melville as letter
writer, Melville and the past, Melville and modernity, Melville's late
writings. The final chapter analyzes Melville scholarship from his day to
ours. Kevin J. Hayes provides comprehensive information about
Melville's life and works in an accessible and engaging book that will be
essential for students beginning to read this important author.

Kevin J. Hayes is Professor of English at the University of Central
Oklahoma. He is the author of many books on Melville and American
literature, including *Melville's Folk Roots* (1999) and the *Checklist of
Melville Reviews* (with Hershel Parker, 1991).

Cambridge Introductions to Literature

This series is designed to introduce students to key topics and authors. Accessible and lively, these introductions will also appeal to readers who want to broaden their understanding of the books and authors they enjoy.

- Ideal for students, teachers, and lecturers
- Concise, yet packed with essential information
- Key suggestions for further reading

Titles in this series:

Eric Bulson   *The Cambridge Introduction to James Joyce*

John Xiros Cooper   *The Cambridge Introduction to T. S. Eliot*

Kirk Curnutt   *The Cambridge Introduction to F. Scott Fitzgerald*

Janette Dillon   *The Cambridge Introduction to Early English Theatre*

Jane Goldman   *The Cambridge Introduction to Virginia Woolf*

Kevin J. Hayes   *The Cambridge Introduction to Herman Melville*

David Holdeman   *The Cambridge Introduction to W. B. Yeats*

M. Jimmie Killingsworth   *The Cambridge Introduction to Walt Whitman*

Ronan McDonald   *The Cambridge Introduction to Samuel Beckett*

Wendy Martin   *The Cambridge Introduction to Emily Dickinson*

Peter Messent   *The Cambridge Introduction to Mark Twain*

John Peters   *The Cambridge Introduction to Joseph Conrad*

Sarah Robbins   *The Cambridge Introduction to Harriet Beecher Stowe*

Martin Scofield   *The Cambridge Introduction to the American Short Story*

Peter Thomson   *The Cambridge Introduction to English Theatre, 1660–1900*

Janet Todd   *The Cambridge Introduction to Jane Austen*

The Cambridge Introduction to
Herman Melville

KEVIN J. HAYES

CAMBRIDGE
UNIVERSITY PRESS

CAMBRIDGE UNIVERSITY PRESS
Cambridge, New York, Melbourne, Madrid, Cape Town, Singapore, São Paulo

Cambridge University Press
The Edinburgh Building, Cambridge CB2 2RU, UK

Published in the United States of America by Cambridge University Press, New York

www.cambridge.org
Information on this title: www.cambridge.org/9780521671040

First published 2007

Printed in the United Kingdom at the University Press, Cambridge

A catalogue record for this publication is available from the British Library

Library of Congress Cataloguing in Publication data
Hayes, Kevin J.
The Cambridge introduction to Herman Melville / by Kevin J. Haye.
   p.   cm. – (Cambridge introductions to literature)
Includes bibliographical references and index.
ISBN-13: 978-0-521-85480-1 (hardback)
ISBN-10: 0-521-85480-6 (hardback)
ISBN-13: 978-0-521-67104-0 (pbk.)
ISBN-10: 0-521-67104-3 (pbk.)
1. Melville, Herman, 1819–1891 – Handbooks, manuals, etc.   2. Authors, American – 19th
century – Biography – Handbooks, manuals, etc.   I. Title.   II. Title: Herman Melville.
III. Series.
PS2386.H35   2007
813'.3 – dc22
[B]
2006025244

ISBN-13 978-0-521-85480-1 hardback
ISBN-13 978-0-521-67104-0 paperback

For Myung-Ran

Contents

Preface

Everybody who has ever read *Moby-Dick* remembers when they first read it. For me, it was the winter of my sophomore year at the University of Toledo. Having yet to declare a major, I enrolled in Professor Hoch's Poe-Hawthorne-Melville seminar with thoughts of majoring in English. Previously, I had read only one Melville work, "Bartleby, the Scrivener," which Mrs Stutz had assigned us in high school English. For the remainder of that school year, Bartleby's catch phrase – "I would prefer not to" – became a part of our classroom banter, but the story itself did not inspire me or exert a lasting influence on my life.

Moby-Dick did.

I still have the books I bought for Professor Hoch's class, which I took – can it be? – almost thirty years ago. We read *Moby-Dick* in the Norton critical edition prepared by Harrison Hayford and Hershel Parker. I have since added many other editions of *Moby-Dick* to my library, but I still cannot bring myself to let go of the first copy I ever owned. Its back is broken, and several pages flutter out every time I open it, but my Norton *Moby-Dick* continues to occupy an important place in my personal library. This is the book that inspired me to devote my life to the study of literature.

It contains underlined passages and marginal comments in three different colors of ink. Each color dates from a different reading. The lengthy comments in red are the most recent: they come from the first time I taught *Moby-Dick* in a Poe-Hawthorne-Melville seminar of my own. The comments in black ink are class notes from a graduate seminar Professor Parker taught at the University of Delaware. (The fact that I was attending graduate school at Delaware further reflects the influence of the Norton *Moby-Dick*: I had decided to study with one of its editors.) The brief marginal comments and the passages underlined in blue ink date from Professor Hoch's undergraduate seminar.

There are noticeable differences in the quality of my marginalia. The red and the black are marks made by a literary professional learning his craft at the start of his career. The marginalia in blue seem amateurish in comparison. They make no notice of plot or narrative technique or characterization or imagery or symbolism. But these early marks do something the later ones do not: they reflect the thrill of discovery. Passages in my copy of *Moby-Dick* underlined in blue represent points of contact, places in the text where Melville had crystallized into words ideas that I had formed only in the vaguest and most inchoate way.

The Cambridge Introduction to Herman Melville gives me the chance to share with others the kind of opportunity I had as an undergraduate, to help readers experience the thrill of discovery that comes from reading Melville for the first time. The four chapters that comprise this book survey Melville's literary career from different perspectives. Chapter 1 tells the story of his life. Using the opening chapter of *Moby-Dick* as a starting point, Chapter 2 introduces the philosophical, historical, and cultural contexts through which to view Melville's writings. This chapter supplies in miniature many ideas that are more fully developed in Chapter 3, which presents a series of critical discussions of his work. And Chapter 4 tells the story of Melville's critical reception, from the contemporary enthusiasm that greeted *Typee* through the near-total neglect he experienced through the Melville revival in the early twentieth century, a time when the world discovered Melville.

Abbreviations

BB   Hayford, Harrison, and Merton M. Sealts, Jr., eds., *Billy Budd, Sailor (An Inside Narrative): Reading Text and Genetic Text*, Chicago: University of Chicago Press, 1962.

CR   Higgins, Brian, and Hershel Parker, eds., *Herman Melville: The Contemporary Reviews*, New York: Cambridge University Press, 1995.

Doubloon   Parker, Hershel, and Harrison Hayford, eds., *Moby-Dick as Doubloon: Essays and Extracts (1851–1970)*, New York: Norton, 1970.

Log   Leyda, Jay, *The Melville Log: A Documentary Life of Herman Melville, 1819–1891*, 1951; reprinted, New York: Gordian Press, 1969.

W   Hayford, Harrison, G. Thomas Tanselle, and Hershel Parker, eds., *The Writings of Herman Melville*, Evanston and Chicago: Northwestern University Press and The Newberry Library, 1968–, 13 vols. to date (1–10, 12, 14–15).

Works   Sadleir, Michael, ed., *The Works of Herman Melville*. London: Constable and Co., 1922–1924, 16 vols.

Chapter 1

Life

Traveling from Pittsfield, Massachusetts to Albany, New York one November to spend Thanksgiving with his family, Herman Melville, at eighteen, had time to reflect on his personal situation. Born in New York City on 1 August 1819, he had enjoyed a comfortable boyhood, but reverses in his father's business during Herman's adolescence had forced the family to relocate to Albany, where his father fared no better. Overambitious schemes and overextended credit took their toll. He died a broken man, leaving his wife Maria and their seven children to fend for themselves. Herman was twelve. His teenage brother Ganesvoort went into business upon their father's death and proved successful until the Depression of 1837 drove him into bankruptcy. To help the family, Herman had left Albany a few months before Thanksgiving this year to teach school in rural Massachusetts.

During the holiday, an uncle gave Herman a copy of John Preston's incongruously titled teachers' manual, *Every Man His Own Teacher*, which supplied the mathematics exercises his students sorely needed. Melville observed that some of them had traveled through their arithmetic "with so great swiftness that they can not recognize objects in the road on a second journey: and are about as ignorant of them as though they had never passed that way before" (*W*, XIV, p. 8). Preston emphasized the nobility of teaching, an endeavor the literary genius typically disdained. The comparison between teaching and writing had the opposite of its intended effect on Melville. Preston's comments are enough to make any teacher with serious literary pretensions wonder what he is doing before a classroom full of unruly students.

Melville had yet to display anything approaching literary genius, but the letter thanking his uncle reveals his predisposition toward the literary life and contains flashes of brilliance. Describing where he lived, Melville indulged his Romantic fancy, situating himself atop "the summit of as savage and lonely a mountain as ever I ascended. The scenery however is most splendid and unusual, – embracing an extent of country in the form of an Ampitheatre sweeping around for many miles and encircling a portion of your state in its compass" (*W*, XIV, p. 8). Portraying the individual within a natural landscape extending to the horizon, Melville offered an image characteristic of the Romantic era and anticipated the figure of Captain Ahab sailing through the vast expanse of the Pacific.

He also said that he was reading and writing to improve himself. J. Orville Taylor's *District School* he studied "to the same advantage, – which a scholar traveling in a country – peruses its hystory, – being surrounded by the scenes it describes." Melville's portrayal of his studying process forms the second figurative use of traveling in this letter. His position as schoolmaster stationed him at the lectern, but his language shows him already "tormented with an everlasting itch for things remote" (*W*, XIV, p. 9; VI, p. 7).

Contemporary writings fostered Melville's curiosity about foreign lands. Never a methodical man, he kept no record of what he read, but his ever-methodical brother Ganesvoort recorded reading much literature, including several articles from *Waldie's Select Circulating Library*, a weekly magazine offering readers selections from the latest literature. Ganesvoort recorded reading John Carne's "Letters from the East," Thomas De Quincey's "Revolt of the Tartars," and Basil Hall's "Schloss Hainfield." *Waldie's* gave the Melville boys a window to an exciting world of foreign adventure.

Herman soon quit teaching and entered Lansingburgh Academy to study surveying and engineering in hopes of qualifying for a position on the Erie Canal. He also flexed his literary muscles. In May 1839, he published two newspaper sketches entitled "Fragments from a writing desk." The tone of these sketches echoes the classic essays of the Augustan age, yet their themes belong to the Romantic era. In "Fragments" Melville created a persona close to yet distinct from himself, a subtle narrative technique he would continue to develop.

Unable to find work on the canal, he signed aboard the *St. Lawrence*, a merchant ship that took him to Liverpool. This early experience influenced his decision to turn whaler. Home from Liverpool, he again taught school briefly before venturing inland to Illinois. Though he left no account of this excursion, numerous references scattered throughout his writings testify to the importance of his journey to "the land-locked heart of our America" (*W*, VI, p. 244). Throughout the trip – down the Erie Canal, through the Great Lakes to Chicago, and overland to Galena – Melville's ever-expansive mind stockpiled images he would use in his writings.

He stayed long enough to see the corn ripen, as "Trophies of Peace: Illinois in 1840" suggests. Despite the subtitle, there is no telling where or when Melville wrote this poem. Even if he wrote it years later, its setting shows he was seeing the Western landscape with a poetic eye. The rows of cornstalks resembled ranks of spear-wielding soldiers. Whereas the battlefield leads to death, the cornfield yields life-giving trophies, heaps of golden grain. The speaker ends by apostrophizing the prairie, urging it to continue its bountiful yield "Though trooper Mars disdainful flout / Nor Annals fame the field" (*Works*, XVI, p. 313).

After leaving Galena, Melville took a riverboat down the Mississippi to Cairo. He recorded his impressions in "The River," a lyrical fragment whose imagery parallels "Trophies of Peace." The first paragraph ends with a question: "In this granary of a continent, this basin of the Mississippi, must not the nations be greatly multiplied and blest?" Once the Missouri River enters the Mississippi, war imagery predominates. The "yellow-painted Missouri" foams "like a Pawnee from ambush." Unlike the Mississippi, the Missouri more nearly resembles "a hostile element than a filial flood" (*W*, X, pp. 497–499). In Melville's hands, the river became a powerful symbol of the violence endemic to America.

The whaling voyage Melville soon undertook would be the most important journey of his life; his inland excursion may be the second most important. Delving into the heart of America before seeing the South Pacific, he created the opportunity to compare locales and recognize what his national geography represented. In Melville's work, the Great Lakes stand for the greatness of America; the prairie represents the nation's natural fecundity; and the Mississippi symbolizes the political, social, and moral complexities facing the nation. The American West embodies the true spirit of the United States. As Melville would say of the Revolutionary patriot Ethan Allan, "His spirit was essentially western; and herein is his peculiar Americanism; for the western spirit is, or will yet be (for no other is, or can be) the true American one" (*W*, VIII, p. 149).

A few months after returning east, Melville signed aboard the *Acushnet*, a whaling vessel which sailed from Massachusetts the first week of January 1841. A year and a half later the *Acushnet* touched at Nukuheva in the Marquesas, where Melville jumped ship with Richard Tobias Greene, whom he immortalized as Toby in *Typee*, the book loosely based on their experiences. After escaping into Nukuheva's lush undergrowth, they traveled overland and ended up among the supposedly cannibalistic Typee natives. Lameness incapacitated Melville; Greene left for help but never returned. Melville remained a few more weeks but eventually signed aboard a passing Australian whaler that brought him to Tahiti, an experience that inspired his second book, *Omoo*. Another whaler brought him to Maui in April 1843.

At Honolulu Melville found work as a pinsetter in a bowling alley. The little known experience may have shaped his personal development significantly. Edgar Allan Poe found philosophy in furniture; Melville, who shared Poe's capacity for seeing ultimate truths in the merest trifles, could have found wisdom in a bowling ball. Like a Mississippi riverboat, the bowling alley is a microcosm of the world where sensitive souls mingle with ne'er-do-wells, a paradoxical place where the raucous sound of tumbling pins induces a mood of quiet contemplation. Melville was not the only important American writer to spend a part of his formative years in a bowling alley.

Hawaii exposed him to a recreational pursuit of a different nature, surfing. There is no indication he attempted to surf himself, but he spent time at Waikiki watching some young Hawaiians surf, which he vividly described in *Mardi*, the earliest instance of surfing in American literature. Melville apparently liked Honolulu well enough to consider settling here, but a bout of homesickness coincided with the arrival of a United States Navy frigate. He impulsively signed on as an ordinary seaman. The frigate cruised the South Pacific and skirted the coastlines of Central and South America but finally reached Boston in October 1844, when Melville was discharged from the navy.

Imagine how he appeared upon returning home. It had been nearly four years since his family had seen him. He was naturally quite handsome. Now twenty-five, physically fit and tanned nut brown, he must have been absolutely striking. During his time away, his older brother had gone through a metamorphosis no less surprising. Ganesvoort Melville had become a famous orator. With the presidential election looming large, he was busy criss-crossing the nation stumping for James K. Polk.

Herman now faced the same problem as when he had left: once more he found himself unemployed. As he awed friends and family members with stories of fantastic adventure in the South Seas, they encouraged him to write up his experiences for publication. To be a professional writer: the thought may not have occurred to him before, but now he found the possibility intriguing. Melville never took long to make a decision. He rapidly made up his mind: he would become a writer.

To get an idea of what to write, he obtained some books describing South Seas adventure that he could use as sources and went to work. When driven, he could write very quickly, an ability he seems to have already possessed as he sat down to write his first book. Having rehearsed the story of *Typee* orally on long, dark nights in the forecastle, he knew his material well. He finished the manuscript within a few months, and Ganesvoort devised a scheme for publishing it.

After his inauguration, President Polk rewarded Ganesvoort for his service on the campaign trail with the secretaryship of the American legation in London. He took Herman's manuscript to England and offered it to John Murray, who thought it too well written to be a sailor's true adventures but accepted it once Ganesvoort assured him of its veracity. Washington Irving read the London edition in proofs and enjoyed it immensely. Upon Irving's recommendation, the American publisher, George P. Putnam accepted the work. Murray issued the work as *Narrative of a Four Months' Residence Among the Natives of a Valley of the Marquesas Islands; or, A Peep at Polynesian Life* (1846). Wiley and Putnam published it as *Typee: A Peep at Polynesian Life*, the title Melville preferred. *Typee* appeared as part of the firm's prestigious new series, Wiley and Putnam's Library of American Books. Sadly, Ganesvoort would not live to enjoy his brother's success. He passed away in London the second week of May 1846.

The American edition brought Herman in contact with series editor Evert Duyckinck, who recruited some of the nation's finest authors as contributors: Margaret Fuller, Nathaniel Hawthorne, Edgar Allan Poe, and William Gilmore Simms. When *Typee* appeared, Duyckinck put copies into the hands of Fuller, Hawthorne, and Simms, all sensitive readers who would be likely to review the book positively. He did not give a copy to Poe, whose caustic reviews had earned him the moniker, "Tomahawk Man."

Many British critics reacted to *Typee* as Murray had. They loved the book's exciting adventure, delightful humor, and fine writing, but they could scarcely believe it was the work of a sailor. Christian Johnstone's reaction is typical. Reviewing the work for an Edinburgh magazine, she observed, "The adventures are very entertaining; so much so, indeed, as to beget a flitting notion that they may sometimes be a little embellished. The style is evidently touched up, or, as masons say, 'pointed' by some literary artist, which also confirms the notion that the story may have been a little coloured." Some questioned whether a person named Herman Melville really existed. Writing a column for a London magazine in July 1847, New York journalist Parke Godwin reassured British readers of Melville's existence: "I saw him in Albany the other day as large as life."[1]

Despite such critical skepticism, *Typee* captured the popular imagination. Not only did it provide informative detail nestled within a suspenseful, yet humorous narrative, it also titillated readers. In an early scene, sailors are greeted by several native women who swim toward them in the nude. The story's love interest, an exotic beauty named Fayaway, thrilled male readers. The recurrence of her name in the popular culture shows how much her character captured the Anglo-American imagination. A steamboat owner in St. Louis christened his vessel *Fayaway*. Multiple British shipowners christened ocean-crossing vessels similarly. And Lord Chesterfield had a horse named Fayaway, which was a favorite at race meets in the 1860s.[2]

Typee was not for male eyes only. The book's exotic quality attracted female readers, too. With tongue partly in cheek, Margaret Fuller said that "sewing societies of the country villages will find this the very book they wish to have read while assembled at their work" (*CR*, p. 38). Lydia Maria Child also enjoyed the book, if her fond reference to Fayaway in "The Hindoo anchorite" is any indication. The details of everyday life among the Typee natives especially interested female readers. Composing a section on personal hygiene for *The Ladies Medical Guide*, Seth Pancoast found *Typee* a useful reference: "We are told by *Melville*, that the Typee girls devote much of their time in arranging their fair and redundant tresses. They bathe several times a day, and anoint their hair with cocoa-nut oil, after each ablution. Melville observes that this oil is fit for the toilet of a queen." Mary Hughs, the creator of Aunt Mary's Library, a popular series of children's books, adapted *Typee* for boys and girls as *May Morning: or, A Visit to the Country*.[3]

The surprising reappearance of Richard Tobias Greene hushed some of the most outspoken critics. Having escaped from Typee valley, he had returned home and settled in Buffalo, New York. Identifying himself as Toby of *Typee*, Greene testified to the book's veracity. He was reunited with Melville, who wrote up the tale of his friend's adventures. Murray published "The Story of Toby" as a pamphlet. The work was appended to subsequent reprintings of *Typee*. There was no convincing some readers. T. K. Hervey complained about the fortuitous reappearance of Toby and the publication of this pamphlet. He observed, "There is a kind of 'handy-dandy' in this mode of presenting the matter – a sort of illogical evidence – a species of affirming in a circle – which increases the puzzle."[4] Hervey had little room to talk. His own modest literary reputation rested on *Australia*, a long poem of South Seas adventure he had written as a student without leaving the safety of Trinity College, Cambridge.

Dedicated to Lemuel Shaw, Chief Justice of the Massachusetts Supreme Court, *Typee* provides a public hint of what was happening privately in Melville's life. During his absence, his older sister Helen had become friends with Judge Shaw's daughter Elizabeth. Upon his return, Melville entered the Shaw family circle. He and Elizabeth fell in love, got engaged, and, after the publication of Melville's second book, *Omoo: A Narrative of Adventures in the South Seas* (1847), got married. They settled in New York City, where Melville resumed work on *Mardi*, the work he had started upon completing *Omoo*.

Typically, Melville would write a short version of a book and then expand it by inserting additional details and reflections derived from his reading. He had used this method with great effectiveness while writing *Typee* and *Omoo*, but his sources for these two books were primarily other narratives of South Seas adventure. During the composition of *Mardi*, he began reading contemplative prose from centuries past, classic texts which influenced *Mardi* profoundly. What started as an adventure story in the manner of *Typee* became a romantic quest, an intellectual odyssey, and a biting political allegory.

Reviews were mixed. Some readers could make no sense of *Mardi*. Its most enthusiastic supporter, Evert Duyckinck reviewed *Mardi: And a Voyage Thither*

(1849) at length. *Mardi* sold poorly, however. Its commercial failure was all the more disappointing because Melville had a growing family to support. The month before *Mardi* appeared Elizabeth had given birth to Malcolm, the first of four children. Her husband could scarcely afford to write books that did not turn a profit.

Melville's situation was not unique. Popularity and literary quality are inversely related. Then as now, the reading public prefers books that meet their expectations. True artists, alternatively, challenge prevailing tastes to advance their art. Having established his reputation with *Typee*, Melville created a set of expectations for his readers, which *Omoo* reaffirmed. When the deliberately difficult *Mardi* challenged contemporary readers, they balked.

Melville wanted to take his art beyond the experimental *Mardi*, to say in print what other authors were afraid to say, but he dashed off two more books based on his personal experiences to be a good provider. His voyage to Liverpool inspired Wellingborough Redburn's adventures in *Redburn, His First Voyage: Being the Sailor-Boy Confessions and Reminiscences of the Son-of-a-Gentleman, in the Merchant Service* (1849), and his naval service inspired *White-Jacket; or, The World in a Man-of-War* (1850). In terms of his creative development, Melville saw their composition as a retrograde movement and referred to both with contempt. *Redburn*, for example, he called "trash" he wrote "to buy some tobacco" (*W*, XV, p. 13). Melville was too hard on himself. Both possess a literary sophistication beyond what he had achieved in either *Typee* or *Omoo*.

Traveling to London to arrange the British publication of *White-Jacket*, Melville immersed himself in the city's literary culture. Soon after arriving, he visited a local reading room, where he saw the latest issue of *Bentley's Miscellany*, which contained an anonymous review of *Redburn*. Robert Bell, who wrote the review, liked *Redburn* better than Melville's earlier works, preferring "a story of living experience" over "dreams of fancy and the excursions of a vivid imagination." Bell apparently kept his authorship secret. He met Melville at a dinner party, but Melville's journal makes no reference to the review's authorship. Bell later read *White-Jacket* and liked it even better than *Redburn*.[5]

Richard Bentley accepted *White-Jacket* and gave its author a substantial advance, but not before Melville had slogged the manuscript through the streets of London searching for a publisher. Otherwise, Melville's London sojourn was delightful. He attended numerous plays and concerts. He visited all the standard tourist destinations – St Paul's, the British Museum, Greenwich Hospital. He dined at the Erechtheum Club and visited the Reform Club. Given his fondness for dark, cozy places, he enjoyed London's pubs the best. One evening he visited the Mitre Tavern in Fleet Street, one of Samuel Johnson's old haunts according to local legend. The Edinburgh Castle – "the beau ideal of a tavern" – was

Melville's favorite. Stopping by one evening with a well-read American friend, he enjoyed "a glorious chop and a pancake, a pint and a half of ale, a cigar and a pipe, and talked high German metaphysics meanwhile" (*W*, XV, p. 19). Why, the Edinburgh Castle served the best Scottish ale he had ever tasted.

Hard by the Edinburgh Castle was Stibbs's Bookshop. What first lured Melville inside was a prominently displayed seventeenth-century folio of *Fifty Comedies and Tragedies* by Francis Beaumont and John Fletcher – "the magnificent, mellow old Beaumont and Fletcher, who have sent the long shadow of their reputation, side by side with Shakspeare's, far down the endless vale of posterity." He bought the book and a Ben Jonson folio, too. He returned for a folio edition of Sir William Davenant's *Works* and a "fine old copy" of Sir Thomas Browne's *Works*. He also managed to coax some complimentary books from Bentley: William Beckford's *Vathek*, William Godwin's *Caleb Williams*, and Mary Shelley's *Frankenstein*. In addition, he purchased copies of Laurence Sterne's *Tristram Shandy* and Thomas De Quincey's *Confessions of an Opium Eater*. Reading De Quincey's *Confessions* the day after buying it, Melville remained indoors by the fire, refusing to see visitors and staying put until he finished this "marvellous book" (*W*, V, p. 168; XV, pp. 44, 47). Looking at what books he acquired in London, one can almost see *Moby-Dick* taking shape.

The time he spent here had a profound impact on Melville. On the city's streets and in its dark, smokey taverns the literature of the past lived. London was a place where seventeenth-century folios could still be had, where the shades of Boswell and Johnson haunted the side streets branching from the Strand, where the writings of Ben Jonson and William Davenant seemed a part of the warp and woof of everyday life. London reminded Melville of a truth his distasteful experiences in the American literary marketplace had obscured: Great writing is something that lasts.

No one can walk away from London unchanged. Its influence on Melville is obvious from the direction his work took. While in London, he scouted locations as he researched *Israel Potter*. Leaving the city, he set aside his plans for this modest historical romance and recovered the literary ambitions he had felt during the composition of *Mardi*. His new book would be an epic of whaling, a *King Lear* of the watery world. For months after returning home in February 1850, he worked intensely on *The Whale*, as he first called the book.

Melville's personal experiences this year reinforced his literary ambitions. On a picnic in the Berkshires, he met Nathaniel Hawthorne, who lived in nearby Lenox. Melville found in Hawthorne a literary soulmate, and the two became fast friends. Always impulsive, Melville borrowed money to buy a farm just north of Pittsfield, which he named Arrowhead after the native artifacts he found there. The numerous farm chores distracted him, but he took inspiration from the nearness of Hawthorne and dedicated *Moby-Dick* to him.

Reviews of *Moby-Dick; or, The Whale* (1851) were disappointing, nay, hurtful. The small-mindedness of the critics stung him. Even Duyckinck, a devout Episcopalian, severely critiqued the book and, in so doing, antagonized Melville, soured their friendship, and adversely affected his next book. Melville avenged the reviewers of *Moby-Dick* within the pages of *Pierre; or, The Ambiguities* (1852). His capacity to write quickly, together with his characteristic impulsiveness, proved a dangerous combination. He added over a hundred more pages to his *Pierre* manuscript, turning his hero into an author midway through the book and making Pierre's frustrations in the literary marketplace a thinly-veiled retelling of his own. But it was the incest plot more than its attack on the literary establishment that antagonized contemporary readers. *Pierre* turned its author into a literary pariah.

Melville could not find a publisher for the next project he completed, a tale of patience and endurance set on an island off the Massachusetts coast entitled *The Isle of the Cross*. He apparently destroyed the manuscript. The recently-discovered fact that Melville completed this work alters the traditional understanding of Melville's life. Typically, biographers have seen *Pierre* as a turning point. Jean-Jacques Mayoux asserted that after writing *Pierre* Melville was "finished, consumed, like Rimbaud after *A Season in Hell.*"[6] No, he was not. He kept working as hard as ever. Unable to find a publisher for *The Isle of the Cross*, Melville changed direction but kept working.

With a resilience that defies easy explanation, he shifted focus and began writing for the magazines. He also completed his long-planned historical novel, *Israel Potter: His Fifty Years of Exile* (1855). Melville's magazine fiction – "prose, as mild and easy as an Indian summer in the woods," Henry James called it – pleased contemporary readers but did little to advance Melville's literary career.[7] He collected several short stories as *The Piazza Tales* (1856). *The Confidence-Man: His Masquerade* (1857), the last novel Melville published in his lifetime, is his most disappointing book, disappointing because it is so good one regrets it is not better. The early chapters recall the Melville of *Moby-Dick* and *Pierre*, an ambitious author unafraid to slay the dragons of a corrupt society, unafraid to offer readers a deliberately difficult book. Having the devil come down to a Mississippi riverboat and assume different guises in the book's early chapters, he forced readers to readjust their focus as each chapter gives way to the next. The first third of the book is an absolute tour de force. Before completing the book, he lost his energy and his direction. Hurriedly completing the manuscript, he did not even stick around to see it through the press. It was after *The Confidence-Man*, not *Pierre*, that Melville was consumed like Rimbaud after *A Season in Hell*.

By the time he brought *The Confidence-Man* to a close, Melville had lost the will, the urge, the energy to write a sequel to the book or, for that matter, to write anything. Since borrowing money to purchase Arrowhead, he had been teetering on the brink of financial disaster, often unable to make the interest payments on the loan and sometimes unable to pay the mortgage. He felt like a failure. His grand dreams of becoming a great writer seemed all but over.

Considering how quickly he could write and realizing that the magazines still welcomed his work, one cannot help but wonder why Melville did not simply dash off a half dozen articles to stave off the wolves. To ask such a question is to ignore his personality and mental state. Melville was one of those rare people, sensitive souls who could penetrate surface reality to see how the world really worked. He looked at his fellow man and saw him with his skin flayed. He could see all the muscles and tendons and sinews that held this frail little thing called man together. But he could penetrate even deeper. His gaze could pierce the darkness of the heart and the depths of the soul. With such insight, Melville recoiled in terror to recognize that such darkness masked moral vacuity. Beneath the surface of man, Melville saw little else beyond duplicity and hypocrisy. How trivial bill collectors and creditors and process servers seem to one who views his fellow man with psychic horror.

Judge Shaw, Melville's practically-minded father-in-law could not understand his son-in-law's horror, but he did know what kind of havoc a creditor could wreak. Shaw rescued him from financial ruin and bankrolled a long recuperative holiday to Europe and the Holy Land. This trip would form the basis for the last great work he published in his lifetime, *Clarel: A Poem and Pilgrimage in the Holy-Land* (1876).

Coming in contact with ancient history and culture during the trip, Melville got a better perspective on the world in which he lived and partly recovered his equanimity. Returning home, however, he faced much the same situation that he had faced upon returning home from the South Pacific as a young man thirteen years earlier: he had to find work. From 1857 through 1859, he earned a modest living on the lecture circuit, but the podium made him uneasy. Unlike Mark Twain, Melville could not transfer his natural tall-tale telling ability to the podium. In his lectures, he assumed a scholarly pose and staunchly refused to caricature himself as the man who had lived among cannibals. He gradually realized that he had neither the talent nor the inclination for public speaking.

During the late 1850s, he began writing verse in a desultory fashion. The Civil War gave his verse renewed focus. He started seeing himself as a modern-day Ossian, a chronicler of the heroes and heroics of the battlefield, but also of the waste and futility of war. He closely followed stories of the war in the newspapers and visited one battlefield to get a firsthand look. He subsequently published *Battle-Pieces and Aspects of War* (1866). The year *Battle-Pieces* appeared, Melville found work as a customs inspector, a profound disappointment for a man who knew he had the talent to rank with the greatest writers in literary history. But he kept writing poetry and issued two brief collections of verse, *John Marr and Other Sailors with some Sea-Pieces* (1888) and *Timoleon* (1891). His late poetry brought him back to prose. He drafted prose headnotes for some of his late poems to put them into context. The works that constitute his unpublished Burgundy Club sketches, for example, began as headnotes to his poetry. And *Billy Budd, Sailor*, his final masterpiece, also began as a headnote to a poem. At the time of his death, 29 September 1891, *Billy Budd* neared completion. Three decades would pass before it saw print.

Chapter 2

Contexts

Introducing himself to the reader in "Loomings," the first chapter of *Moby-Dick*, Ishmael feels compelled to explain why he goes to sea. As he does so, he gradually reveals his personality and his characteristic thought process. He is someone who examines any given subject from every possible angle. He contextualizes his decision to go to sea so broadly that the chapter provides a useful framework for understanding the philosophical, historical, and cultural contexts of *Moby-Dick* and, indeed, Herman Melville's work as a whole. Overall, "Loomings" suggests many different ways of looking at Melville's writings.

The existential context

In the chapter's initial paragraph, Ishmael asserts that going to sea gives him a way to preserve his very existence. Despite the weightiness of this assertion, Ishmael conveys the idea in a light-hearted manner. He describes the malaise that sometimes overcomes him on land and his ensuing compulsion to step into the street and methodically knock people's hats off. Given his humorous tone, readers may be unsure how seriously they should take what Ishmael says. At face value, his words suggest that if he could not sail the ocean, he would surely kill himself. Going to sea he calls his "substitute for pistol and ball" (*W*, VI, p. 3). The ocean supplies Ishmael's existential context. Without the escape it offers, suicide would be his only way out.

Though humor mitigates the seriousness of what Ishmael says, it does not detract from the significance of what Melville was saying. "Loomings" anticipates something E. M. Cioran would say in *The Temptation to Exist*. Whatever excuses, reasons, or fictions we create to justify our existence have value. The conscious decision to abjure suicide is akin to an act of religious faith. To avoid self-annihilation, everyone must find an existential context – or imagine one. The sea is Ishmael's. And, he implies, most men share a similar attitude toward the sea whether they realize it or not: "If they but knew it, almost all men in their degree, some time or other, cherish very nearly the same feelings towards the ocean with me" (*W*, VI, p. 3).

Melville did not hesitate to let readers know that he was dealing with big, important ideas, ideas as fundamental as those involving man's reason to exist. Incorporating such ideas from the first chapter of *Moby-Dick*, he showed that this was no ordinary sea story. His willingness to grapple with life-and-death issues constitutes a defining characteristic of Melville's writings. Other works provide further examples. The title character of *Pierre*, for instance, views life in absolute terms. Trying to choose a course of action in the face of unprecedented personal crisis, Pierre Glendinning contrasts behavior acceptable in the real world with behavior that might be acceptable in an ideal world. Tragically, he resolves to live according to the ideal world regardless of the consequences in the real. Further examples could be drawn from *Clarel* and *Billy Budd*. Melville's most ambitious works dare to question man's place on earth.

The historical context

Developing his comparison between suicide and the sea, Ishmael finds a classical allusion appropriate: "With a philosophical flourish Cato throws himself upon his sword; I quietly take to the ship" (*W*, VI, p. 3). Melville's complex allusion refers to Cato, a figure from antiquity who stabbed himself to death instead of submitting to Caesar's tyrannical rule. A favorite figure in Revolutionary America, Cato was often associated with Patrick Henry, who, Cato-like, pretended to stab himself at the end of his famous exclamation, "Give me liberty or give me death!" (Liberty was Patrick Henry's existential context.) In Melville's day, schoolboys often memorized Henry's speech and mimicked his behavior. With one reference, Melville invoked the classical era and the Revolutionary American past.

Melville's fascination with ancient Greece and Rome grew as his writing developed. In 1849, he acquired a copy of the thirty-seven-volume edition of the *Harper's Family Classical Library*, a major purchase that allowed him to deepen his knowledge of classical history, literature, and mythology. He soon put the work to use: many of the classical allusions in *Redburn* can be traced to this multivolume work.[1] Through the rest of his life, stories from the ancients became increasingly important to him. Ten years later a visitor to Arrowhead found Melville "soured by criticism and disgusted with the civilized world and with our Christendom in general and in particular. The ancient dignity of Homeric times afforded the only state of humanity, individual or social, to which he could turn with any complacency" (*Log*, II, p. 605). In his mind, Melville idealized the ancient past, seeing it as a place free from the peccadillos that beset the creative artist in the modern age. Filled with classical references and characters, *Timoleon* shows that Melville continued to indulge his fascination with antiquity at the end of his life.

In terms of the American past, the Revolutionary era exerted an important influence on Melville from his childhood. His grandfather Major Thomas Melvill (as the family name was originally spelled) was a hero of the Revolution who participated in the Boston Tea Party. The family even retained a vial containing tea leaves from that fateful evening. His grandfather on his mother's side, General Peter Ganesvoort, was a Revolutionary hero, too. In charge of Fort Stanwix in 1777, he successfully defended it against a British siege that lasted nearly three weeks. Thereafter General Peter Ganesvoort was known as the Hero of Fort Stanwix.

History was most important to Melville when he could personally link himself to it, and he was proud of his heroic heritage. His family pride, however, did not necessarily compel him to celebrate heroism or patriotism in his writings. His references to the American Revolution are often ironic. *Israel Potter*, the historical novel he set during the Revolutionary War, tells the story of a little known American patriot neglected by the United States and exiled in London for forty years. George Washington appears in Melville's writings numerous times – but not as a hero. Rather, he functions as a touchstone for the common man. Instead of elevating Washington, Melville brought him down to street level, equating him with humbler souls to show the essential humanity of all men.

The urban context

While explaining the universal allure of the sea, Ishmael uses the people of Manhattan as examples to prove his point. It is important to realize that

Moby-Dick, this classic tale of adventure on the high seas, begins in New York City. Explaining the hypnotic allure of water, Ishmael describes the character-istic behavior of New Yorkers. During times of leisure, they flock to the outer edges of this island city. On any given Sunday afternoon "stand thousands upon thousands of mortal men fixed in ocean reveries. Some leaning against the spiles; some seated upon the pier-heads; some looking over the bulwarks of ships from China; some high aloft in the rigging, as if striving to get a still better seaward peep" (*W*, VI, p. 4). Here, Ishmael assumes the role of what Henri Lefebvre would call a rhythmanalyst. Seeking to understand the rhythms of the city, the rhythmanalyst examines the relationship of time and behavior and recognizes how people move through the urban environment.[2] Identifying differences between the workaday behavior of New Yorkers and their leisure behavior, Ishmael attunes himself to their rhythms and is able to imagine what they are thinking.

The people of Manhattan, daydreamers all, look toward the sea, imagining where they could be instead of where they are. The city is a prison, and the water provides the only means of escape. Like the sea, the city has a rhythm all its own. Seen in terms of physical space, however, the city and the ocean are virtual opposites. The city, even the biggest of cities, remains a severely limited space. The ocean, alternatively, seems boundless. Leaving the city and going to sea is akin to setting the mind free and letting it soar, as Chapter 23 of *Moby-Dick*, "The Lee Shore," beautifully suggests. In this chapter, Ishmael observes that "in landlessness alone resides the highest truth, shoreless, indefinite as God" (*W*, VI, p. 107).

Though much of Melville's fiction is set far from land, cities remain impor-tant to his work. *Omoo* contains no cities per se, but the city forms a frequent point of reference. The book's humor, for example, largely stems from the fact that Melville's narrator behaves as a citified dandy while island hopping in the South Pacific. The time Wellingborough Redburn spends in poverty-stricken Liverpool marks his introduction to the horrors of the modern city, an initia-tion which coincides with his entry to adulthood. Pierre Glendinning's decision to leave the country for the city accelerates his tragic downward spiral. Several of Melville's short stories are set in cities, too. "Bartleby, the Scrivener," the most modern of his tales, occurs in Wall Street and reveals like no other work before Stephen Crane's *Maggie, a Girl of the Streets* the coldness and anonymity of the modern city.

Incorporating the squalid living conditions in the tenements of New York, Crane would make imaginative use of rookeries, that is the old churches, man-sions, and warehouses that had been partitioned into separate apartments to house multiple families in a single dwelling. The term rookery suggests that the city was transforming people into animals, a notion that would become prevalent among the realist and naturalist writers of the late nineteenth century. The partitioning of these wonderful old buildings began in Melville's day, however. Impoverished and unwelcome in New York society, Pierre Glendinning moves into the Church of the Apostles, a rookery formed from an old church subdivided into numerous apartments. In "Jimmy Rose," one of the pieces of magazine fiction Melville published in the mid 1850s, the narrator inherits "a great old house in a narrow street of one of the lower wards, once the haunt of style and fashion, full of gay parlors and bridal chambers; but now, for the most part, transformed into counting-rooms and warehouses. There bales and boxes usurp the place of sofas; day-books and ledgers are spread where once the delicious breakfast toast was buttered. In those old wards the glorious old soft-waffle days are over" (*W*, IX, p. 336). Melville's New York fiction documents the passing of the old city and the development of the new. In his portrayal of the city, he anticipates the themes and concerns of realist fiction.

The visual context

The development of the city and the rise of modern visual culture are inseparable. The two come together in the flaneur, a figure who took the city streets as his natural habitat. Indulging in his characteristic behavior, the flaneur combined walking, looking, and thinking. The place where the flaneur typically walked and looked and thought was a city's shop-lined boulevard. The flaneur was a manifestation of the modern city, and Melville made significant use of flanerie in his writings. Previous observers have hesitated to use the word flaneur when discussing Melville's work, but the term first entered English usage shortly before Melville turned professional writer, and it appears in the critical discourse before *Moby-Dick* appeared.

The words Ishmael uses to encourage his readers to look around Manhattan reflect the defining activities of the flaneur: "Circumambulate the city of a dreamy Sabbath afternoon. Go from Corlears Hook to Coenties Slip, and from thence, by Whitehall, northward. What do you see?" Melville reemphasized the importance of walking and looking in some of his other works. The narrator of "Poor man's pudding and rich man's crumbs" also assumes the role of flaneur. Describing his reasons for visiting London, he states, "I come but to roam and see." Describing his attitude toward walking around the city he explains, "I wandered about for the best reception an adventurous traveler can have – the reception, I mean, which unsolicited chance and accident throw in his venturous way" (*W*, VI, p. 4; IX, pp. 297–298). Such randomness formed another important aspect of the flaneur's urban rambles. The leisurely pace of the flaneur also influenced the narrative pace of *The Confidence-Man*, which "moves with a kind of loose artifice, a *boulevardier's* gait, through its succession of dialogues."[3]

For the flaneur, the act of seeing as he walks the city streets resembles the reading process. The urban landscape, with its storefronts, its people, its billboards and street signs, is something to be read and studied. Walking slowly, the flaneur gradually forms an interpretation of what he sees. As Walter Benjamin observed, the flaneur "composes his reverie as text to accompany the images."[4]

Flanerie was just one manifestation of a set of interrelated aspects of nineteenth-century visual culture. The flaneur has been called the physiognomist of the street. This epithet links flanerie with physiognomy, the art of judging character and disposition according to facial features. In the late eighteenth century, Johann Caspar Lavater codified the practice of physiognomy. Lavater's textbook, *Essays on Physiognomy*, was reprinted dozens of times, and Melville acquired a copy in 1849 (*W*, XV, p. 24). Much as the flaneur could read the urban streets, the physiognomist could read a person's face. Phrenology is closely related to physiognomy. It, too, involves reading exterior signs to interpret what is within. Instead of reading the face to determine personality, the phrenologist reads the bumps on the skull.

Flanerie, phrenology, and physiognomy are all based on the notion that exterior signs enable the observer to discern what lies beneath the surface. Describing a physiognomy manual in *Pierre*, Aunt Dorothea explains that the book laid down "the strangest and shadowiest rules . . . for detecting people's innermost secrets by studying their faces." While in London, the narrator of "The two temples" encounters a tattered little girl passing out handbills whose "strange skill in physiognomy" allows her to instantly determine that the narrator is penniless (*W*, VII, p. 79; IX, p. 311). The behavior of Melville's tattered girl implies that experience and necessity can heighten a person's ability to read the faces of others. From *Typee* to *Billy Budd*, Melville indulged his fascination with physiognomy, though he was never completely convinced of its validity. Given his intuitive knowledge of man's innate evil, Melville knew that some faces would always remain unreadable texts.

Melville's ambivalence toward physiognomy and phrenology helps explain his belligerence toward another aspect of modern visual culture, the photograph. During the 1840s, daguerreotype portraiture became quite popular, and steel-engraved portraits based on daguerreotypes became a prevalent form of magazine illustration. Often, authors' portraits accompanied their periodical contributions. Generally disliking all forms of publicity, Melville found portraits derived from photographs particularly insidious. They gave people the opportunity to phrenologize by proxy. Instead of judging authors by what they wrote, readers could judge them by how they appeared in magazine illustrations. Melville refused to have his photograph taken for a long time. He well understood that the words he put on the page provided a much better indication of his mind than the bumps nature put on his skull.

Despite his animosity toward the photograph, Melville experimented with many innovative visual techniques in his writings. "Norfolk Isle and the Chola widow," the finest of the ten sketches set on the Galapagos Islands that comprise "The Encantadas," provides a good example of his visual sensibilities. Temporarily living on Norfolk Isle to hunt tortoises with her husband and brother, a woman named Hunilla watches the two men venture to sea in their boat one day. Horrified, she sees their boat sink and both men perish, leaving her widowed and stranded. Melville wrote:

> The real woe of this event passed before her sight as some sham tragedy on the stage. She was seated on a rude bower among the withered thickets, crowning a lofty cliff, a little back from the beach. The thickets were so disposed, that in looking upon the sea at large she peered out from among the branches as from the lattice of a high balcony. But upon the day we speak of here, the better to watch the adventure of those two hearts she loved, Hunilla had withdrawn the branches to one side, and held them so. They formed an oval frame, through which the bluely boundless sea rolled like a painted one. And there, the invisible painter painted to her view the wave-tossed and disjointed raft, its once level logs slantingly upheaved, as raking masts, and the four struggling arms undistinguishable among them; and then all subsided into smooth-flowing creamy waters, slowly drifting the splintered wreck; while first and last, no sound of any sort was heard. Death in a silent picture; a dream of the eye; such vanishing shapes as the mirage shows.   (*W*, IX, p. 154)

Unaware that this passage was written in the mid 1850s, one might suppose it comes from the age of cinema. Describing a spectator watching moving images through a frame, Melville anticipated the invention of motion pictures. He was doing in words what filmmakers would do in celluloid four decades later. Though the technology of the moving image had yet to evolve, the discourse of the moving image, as Melville's words suggests, was starting to emerge. Some of his other works similarly reflect Melville's prescient visual sensibilities. Of all the world's great novels, Eric Rohmer observed, *Moby-Dick* "is the one that best displays the type of beauty that the screen is most able to highlight . . .

this novel is already a true film."[5] Melville's affinity with the cinema also helps explain why film references work so well to gloss his writings.

The psychological context

Melville's fascination with visual culture extends backwards as well as forwards. He was especially intrigued with an age-old visual phenomenon: the reflection. Developing his ideas about man's fascination with water, Ishmael brings in another classical figure for example, Narcissus. Unable to "grasp the tormenting, mild image he saw in the fountain," Narcissus "plunged into it and was drowned. But that same image, we ourselves see in all rivers and oceans. It is the image of the ungraspable phantom of life; and this is the key to it all" (*W*, VI, p. 5).

Melville's use of Narcissus not only reinforces the importance of the classical past to his thought, it also shows his anticipation of modern psychological thought. Narcissism would become a major impulse in Freudian thought. Including a reference to Narcissus in the first chapter of *Moby-Dick*, Melville revealed the importance of psychological motivation to the story. Like Narcissus, everyone must ultimately confront the self. Physiognomy may be a sham. Phrenology may be a sham. In other words, it may be impossible for us to read the faces of others and know what they are thinking. Melville's reference to Narcissus elicits a more fundamental question: To what extent can individuals read their own images? Are there aspects of ourselves hidden from our view?

In a desultory way, *Mardi* explores many different psychological motivations. *Moby-Dick* on the other hand concentrates on one particular mental affliction, monomania. This psychological term had entered the English language not long before Melville began writing. With his portrayal of Captain Ahab, Melville created the most detailed portrait of a monomaniac ever created. Not all readers have been satisfied with Melville's depiction of Ahab's madness. Henry Nash Smith, for one, found a weakness in its portrayal: Melville never fully developed Ahab's early psychological motivations.[6]

Melville himself realized that there was much more he could say as he explored a character's motivation. The weakness Smith found in *Moby-Dick* Melville remedied in *Pierre*, the greatest psychological novel in American literature before Henry James. Melville carefully explored the motivations underlying Pierre's behavior. Pierre understands many of them, but there are some psychological motivations hidden from his view. Ungraspable phantoms haunt Pierre, too. Melville used similar language to say so: "He felt that what he had always before considered the solid land of veritable reality, was now being audaciously encroached upon by bannered armies of hooded phantoms, disembarking in his soul, as from flotillas of specter-boats" (*W*, VII, p. 49). Several of Melville's subsequent works – "Bartleby, the scrivener," "Benito Cereno," *Billy Budd* – explore other aspects of the psyche.

The American context

Though Ishmael starts with the island of Manhattan to illustrate the fascination with water that people share, he quickly expands his geographical scope to span North America. He explains that contemplative souls across the continent are drawn to water: "Should you ever be athirst in the great American desert, try this experiment, if your caravan happen to be supplied with a metaphysical professor. Yes, as every one knows, meditation and water are wedded for ever." Dissatisfied with only one example, he presents others, asking his readers: "Were Niagara but a cataract of sand, would you travel your thousand miles to see it? Why did the poor poet of Tennessee, upon suddenly receiving two handfuls of silver, deliberate whether to buy him a coat, which he sadly needed, or invest his money in a pedestrian trip to Rockaway Beach?" (*W*, VI, pp. 4–5). These geographical references are the earliest of many American place names that fill the pages of *Moby-Dick* and reinforce the book's uniquely American quality.

While taking the story from New England to the Pacific, Ishmael continually makes comparisons between ocean and prairie. Such comparisons were not unusual, but the extent of them in *Moby-Dick* is extraordinary.[7] As the story of a hunt, *Moby-Dick* parallels numerous hunting tales that were so much a part of American literature and folklore. Ishmael frequently compares the whale hunt with the hunt for buffalo. And ultimately the Pacific Ocean is an analogue for the American West. As Charles Olson observed, Melville was "long-eyed enough to understand the Pacific as part of our geography, another West, prefigured in the Plains, antithetical."[8] Much as Americans were bound to cross the continent, they were bound and determined to span the globe.

Moby-Dick was written during a time of literary jingoism. The magazines of the day were filled with manifestoes clamoring for great American literature. If the United States is the greatest country in the world, the argument went, then it should have the greatest literature in the world. During the composition of *Moby-Dick*, Melville himself wrote a magazine article that contributed to, even as it spoofed, the jingoistic manifestoes of his day. "Hawthorne and his Mosses," ostensibly a review of Nathaniel Hawthorne's *Mosses from an Old Manse*, also clamors for great American literature and suggests that America was close to producing an author the caliber of Shakespeare.

Conscious of his responsibility as an American author, Melville explored the national character in other works. Israel Potter may be his fullest manifestation of the American national character, but the historical figures Potter meets during his adventures – Benjamin Franklin, John Paul Jones, Ethan Allen – illuminate other aspects of the national character. In "Benito Cereno," Captain Amasa Delano exemplifies American naiveté. Boarding Cereno's vessel unaware that it has been overtaken by slaves, Delano shows how easily the American walks into danger oblivious of the consequences. As his various writings indicate, Melville was fascinated with what being an American meant.

Melville's interest in the meaning of America shows up even in his most ephemeral writings. Into his copy of William Hazlitt's *Table Talk* he pasted an article clipped from a newspaper discussing the relationship between leisure and knowledge. Melville's precise source has so far gone unnoticed, but the clipping comes from an article about the Birmingham and Midland Institute in the London *Times* (4 October 1862). In this article, Melville partly underlined the following passage: "Leisure is the nurse of art and scholarship, the gradual untier of knots, the guide that ushers into the depth and mysteries of knowledge, the gradual former of the discrimination and perception which distinguishes the man of high education." Directly beneath this clipping he wrote, "How un-American is all this, and yet – *how true.*"[9] The fast-paced lifestyle was already an established aspect of American culture. From Melville's perspective, it was adversely affecting the nation's intellectual life.

The context of labor

Not only does Ishmael explain why he goes to sea in "Loomings," he also explains how. He goes "as a simple sailor, right before the mast, plumb down into the forecastle, aloft there to the royal mast-head" (*W*, VI, pp. 5–6). Aboard a sailing vessel, the mast marked the dividing line between sailors and officers. Emphasizing that he sailed before the mast, Ishmael proves himself to be a hard-working crew member. And *Moby-Dick* constitutes one of the finest stories of working life ever written. Charles Burchfield especially enjoyed Melville's description of the sailors as they chased whales, which made him wonder whether man must perform hard physical labor to enjoy the world. In *Moby-Dick*, C. L. R. James observed, Melville "painted a body of men at work, the skill and the danger, the laboriousness and the physical and mental mobilization of human resources, the comradeship and the unity, the simplicity and the naturalness." The crew members are the real heroes of *Moby-Dick*, James continued. Their heroism "consists in their everyday doing of their work."[10]

Moby-Dick, of course, was not the first time Melville depicted the plight of workers on the seas. In *Typee*, Tommo and Toby jump ship to escape their captain's brutal rule. In *Omoo*, the sailors protest against their abuse, letting themselves be carried off their ship in leg irons rather than submitting to the captain's tyranny. *Redburn* minutely depicts life aboard a merchant vessel. And *White-Jacket* portrays the abuses that sailors in the United States Navy experience in a way that anticipates Sergei Eisenstein's *Battleship Potemkin*. It is unsurprising that Marxists like James and Eisenstein should be drawn to his work: Melville was the first major novelist to make the worker his hero.

The context of slavery

It is impossible to consider the labor situation in Melville's America without taking slavery into consideration. Any American writing in 1850 could scarcely ignore what slavery was doing to the nation. In "Loomings," Ishmael makes a brief reference to slavery as he elaborates the sailor's workaday world: "What of it, if some old hunks of a sea-captain orders me to get a broom and sweep down the decks? What does that indignity amount to, weighed, I mean, in the scales of the New Testament? Do you think the archangel Gabriel thinks anything the less of me, because I promptly and respectfully obey that old hunks in that particular instance? Who aint a slave? Tell me that" (*W*, VI, p. 6). The attitude Ishmael holds toward slavery differs greatly from that held by the abolitionists of Melville's day. To what extent do Ishmael's words reflect Melville's own attitude?

Battle-Pieces clarifies Melville's vehement opposition to slavery. In the prose supplement that closes this collection of Civil War verse, he wrote, "Those of us who always abhorred slavery as an atheistical iniquity, gladly we join in the exulting chorus of humanity over its downfall" (*Works*, XVI, p. 186). In his writings before the war, Melville never assumed the role of polemicist. Not even in "Benito Cereno," his fullest treatment of slavery, did he launch a diatribe against its practice. Melville eschewed abolitionist rhetoric. It has become cliche to call slavery the great national sin. Melville took a much broader view. Instead of seeing slavery as unique to African descendants in the United States, he saw it as a universal condition that could afflict anyone. Whoever lets someone or something control their behavior becomes a slave.

Another unusual reference to slavery occurs in "The Paradise of Bachelors and the Tartarus of Maids." Traveling to a local paper mill, the narrator of this story watches the women operating the machinery. They remain silent as their machine emits a low, steady hum: "Machinery – that vaunted slave of humanity – here stood menially served by human beings, who served mutely and cringingly as the slave serves the Sultan. The girls did not so much seem accessory wheels to the general machinery as mere cogs to the wheels" (*W*, IX, p. 328). These words could serve as a gloss on Ishmael's who-aint-a-slave query. The invention of industrial machinery was supposed to free mankind from demeaning manual labor. Instead, it seems to have switched roles, becoming master to those who worked it. For Melville, slavery was not just a national disgrace: it was metaphor that symbolized many different forms of oppression.

The world context

Whereas numerous topical and geographical references brand *Moby-Dick* as an American book, Melville situated the work in terms of world events, too. Ishmael nestles his whaling voyage between a "Grand Contested Election for the Presidency of the United States" and a "Bloody Battle in Affghanistan" (*W*, VI, p. 7). Of course, Melville was using irony to place the voyage of this lowly whaleman amidst major events of national and international importance. Yet Ishmael's words are not totally ironic. There is an interconnectedness between events both great and small that cannot be easily separated without detriment to the whole. The battle Ishmael mentioned, for example, eerily foreshadows his personal fate.

During the Khoord Kabul battle of 1842, a column of 16,000 British troops retreating from Afghanistan was ambushed in the pass between Kabul and Jallalabad. Only one British soldier reached the garrison at Jallalabad alive.[11] The similarity between the fate of these British troops and the fate of Ishmael's fellow sailors aboard the *Pequod* conveys history's tendency to repeat itself. The reference to this battle in "Loomings" broadens the interpretive possibilities of *Moby-Dick* considerably. The voyage of the *Pequod* represents any dangerous journey mankind may undertake. Ultimately, it symbolizes man's sojourn on earth.

The imaginative context

In the final paragraph of "Loomings," Ishmael provides one last reason to explain why he goes to sea. This reason is much less tangible than his earlier ones. In the end, he goes because "the great flood-gates of the wonder-world swung open, and in the wild conceits that swayed me to my purpose, two and two there floated into my inmost soul, endless processions of the whale, and, midmost of them all, one grand hooded phantom, like a snow hill in the air" (*W*, VI, p. 7). In short, the superstition-filled legends of great whales and the story of one legendary whale in particular motivated him to go to sea as a whaler. When it came down to it, the power of story on Ishmael's imagination motivates him more than anything. He goes to see because he longs to enter the world of imagination it represents. Reading Melville, we, too, enter the world of imagination, a world more boundless than the vast Pacific.

Writings

Herman Melville created a rich and diverse body of work unparalleled in American literature. No single approach can plumb the depths of his writing, but a multifaceted approach may provide a way to begin understanding their complexities. Organized chronologically, this lengthy chapter is subdivided into twelve sections. Some discuss individual works. Others link multiple works together according to common themes.

Typee, the work that established Melville's reputation, gets its own section. *Moby-Dick, Pierre,* and *Billy Budd,* generally recognized as his three finest works, also receive sections of their own. *Omoo, Battle-Pieces,* and *Clarel,* Melville's three most neglected works, are treated separately in an effort to recognize writings that have never received their just desserts. Years ago Lewis Mumford called *Omoo* "the most underrated of Melville's books," observing that it is typically "treated as if it were but the rinsings of the heady Typeean jug."[1] Mumford's comments still apply. *Omoo* has yet to get the attention it deserves. The discussion of it here attempts to remedy such neglect. College anthologies typically include a few selections from *Battle-Pieces*, but the poems that comprise *Battle-Pieces* deserve to be read in their entirety and in consecutive order to experience the book's tremendous power.

Few readers have the patience for *Clarel*. Writing fifty years after Melville published the poem, John Freeman observed, "Descriptive verse is no longer in vogue, and the cinema has usurped whatever place it retained until the twentieth century; and it is scarcely too much to say that, as to a large part of *Clarel*'s purpose, it is fulfilled more admirably by the cinema."[2] While a five-hundred-page poem may seem even more out of place now than it did in Freeman's time, *Clarel* amply repays the effort required to read it. The discussion of it in this chapter emphasizes its importance to American literature by situating *Clarel* within the tradition of the modern American verse epic, a tradition which extends from Walt Whitman's *Song of Myself* through Ezra Pound's *Cantos* and William Carlos Williams's *Paterson*.

The other sections in this chapter treat multiple works together according to different themes. At the risk of minimizing their individual significance, *Mardi*, *Redburn*, and *White-Jacket* are discussed together in a single section. *Mardi*, Melville's most ambitious work before *Moby-Dick*, is also his least satisfying aesthetically. Much less ambitious, *Redburn* and *White-Jacket* nonetheless show how Melville learned narrative control. Taken together, all three show Melville in the process of learning how to become a great writer.

Melville's letters have never been taken seriously as literature, but they deserve to be. The section following the discussion of *Pierre* takes several of Melville's private letters for example to show how he excelled as a letter writer. In many ways, he was more comfortable writing private letters to sympathetic correspondents than writing books destined for the sometimes insensitive reading public.

Two complementary sections look at Melville's depiction of the past and his anticipation of the future. The first, which discusses *Israel Potter* and "Benito Cereno," examines how Melville rewrote his source material to suit the times in which he was writing. In each case, Melville took decades-old personal narratives and refashioned them into insightful stories told from the third-person. The next section looks at Melville's understanding of the modern world as reflected in "The Lightning-Rod Man," *The Confidence-Man*, and "Bartleby, the Scrivener." Another section treats his Burgundy Club book and other late writings to show how they reflect his personal concerns and influenced his last great work, *Billy Budd*.

The faces of *Typee*

Reading an old Liverpool guidebook, Wellingborough Redburn finds that its "brief and reverential" preface makes it seem "as if the writer were all the time bowing." Melville obviously thought a book's preface should work differently. Of course it should introduce the author to the reader, but it should not do so in an obsequious manner. He had already formed a good idea how to write a preface before *Redburn*. In the preface to *Typee*, he cheerfully introduces himself without bowing. Instead, he appears mildly confrontational as he establishes an opposition between sailors like himself and his stay-at-home readers – "fire-side people" he calls them. Occurrences that seem beyond belief to them are "as common-place as a jacket out at elbows" to the world-wandering sailor (*W*, IV, p. 146; I, p. xiii).

By definition a preface puts a face onto the front of a book. With *Typee*, Melville never put a name to the face. Told in the first person, the book is ostensibly narrated by him, but the preface is unsigned. Beyond the title page, his name appears nowhere in the text of this personal narrative. Since the Typee natives cannot pronounce the name of the book's first-person narrator, he goes by a name they can pronounce, Tommo. The persona of Tommo is a guise Melville assumes, a mask allowing him to tell a fictionalized story yet claim it as truth. Before the preface ends, Tommo sounds more like one of Melville's later fictional characters, the shape-shifting Confidence Man. Assuring readers that the story he is about to tell is true, Tommo hopes that "his anxious desire to speak the unvarnished truth will gain for him the confidence of his readers" (*W*, I, p. xiv).

As the story develops, the word "confidence" occurs twice more with much the same meaning. Disgruntled by the sailor's life, Tommo and fellow crew member Toby jump ship at Nukuheva. While it is sometimes difficult to separate *Typee* fact from *Typee* fiction, in Toby Greene's case, Melville's depiction coincides with independent testimony. Writing in the Buffalo *Morning Express* (14 March 1855), an acquaintance characterized Greene as "a whole-hearted, genial, companionable gentleman, full of frankness, amiability, and jollity." Together they escape overland and undergo many dangerous yet sometimes hilarious adventures before reaching an unknown valley.

As they enter the mysterious valley, they remain unaware whether it is the land of the reputedly innocuous Happar or that of the reputedly cannibalistic Typee. Descending into the populated part of the valley much as Satan enters the Garden of Eden in *Paradise Lost*, they first encounter a naked, amorous young couple. Nearly exhausting his knowledge of their native tongue, Tommo utters a few phrases and secures from them "a little confidence" (*W*, I, p. 68). Echoing the preface, this phrase parallels Tommo's first contact with the Typee and his first contact with the reader. Both Typee natives and contemporary readers are alien to Tommo, a youthful American sailor and an inexperienced author. To befriend either group, he must secure their confidence.

The word "confidence" recurs as Tommo and Toby discuss the communal identity of the natives they have encountered. Are they Typee or Happar? Toby assures him they are Happar, but his assurance comes with what Tommo calls "a show of confidence which was intended to disguise his doubts" (*W*, I, p. 69). Tommo's words reveal the complexity of his situation. Though he wishes to secure the confidence of the natives, he understands that confidence is something that can be feigned. Sharing a common culture with his shipmate, Tommo can tell when Toby is feigning confidence. Will he be able to read the faces of those from another culture as easily? Will he be able to tell what the natives are thinking solely by their expressions?

Physiognomy maintained that exterior signs enable shrewd observers to discern the person within, the man behind the mask. It is one thing to read the face of a person who shares a similar cultural heritage; it is something else entirely to read the face of a person from a different culture. The possibility, or impossibility, of reading others on the basis of their physical appearance forms a central theme of *Typee*. Tommo looks into the faces of the islanders to see who they are and what they are thinking. They look back at him and do the same.

Once within the native village, Tommo and Toby come before a council of chiefs. One chief – Mehevi – looks at Tommo with a "rigidity of aspect" that sends shivers through him. Mehevi "never once opened his lips," Tommo observes, "but maintained his severe expression of countenance, without turning his face aside for a single moment. Never before had I been subjected to so strange and steady a glance; it revealed nothing of the mind of the savage, but it appeared to be reading my own" (*W*, I, p. 71). Tommo fears Mehevi, not because he sees anger or displeasure or danger in his face, but because he sees nothing. Tommo cannot initially penetrate the native visage. Mehevi's face is an unreadable text, and its unreadability is what terrifies Tommo.

Curious to see the foreigners, numerous Typee villagers file past them to get a better look. In Tommo's words, the natives "bathed themselves in the light of our benignant countenances" (*W*, I, p. 77). The phrase "benignant countenances" recurs frequently in the contemporary discourse. Though it literally indicates personal benevolence, it was sometimes used ironically to denote an overinflated, self-righteous sense of superiority. Melville's use of the phrase parallels Tommo's presence in Typee with the presence of other Westerners in the South Pacific islands, the missionaries. But his tone is facetious. Elsewhere in the narrative, Tommo excoriates the missionaries for imposing Western beliefs and values onto the South Pacific islanders. In this passage, Melville humorously exaggerates the influence of the white man's face upon the swarthy-visaged islanders to the point of absurdity. Frederick Douglass's owner looked upon him with a "benignant countenance," too.[3]

Acclimating themselves to their new surroundings, Tommo and Toby join the household of Marheyo, a kindly, well-respected village elder. Gradually they learn more about his people, who turn out to be Typee, not Happar. As Tommo describes the Typee valley, it seems like utopia. Walt Whitman compared *Typee* to Simon Berington's *Memoirs of Sigr Gaudentio di Lucca*, an eighteenth-century utopian novel which describes an imaginary place in Africa characterized by political and social harmony (*CR*, p. 46). To his relief, Tommo initially sees no evidence of cannibalism, but he still has much to learn about his hosts. The process he undergoes as he attempts to discern their character is akin to the process of reading a book, a comparison made explicit by his description of Kory-Kory, his man Friday. Kory-Kory's body, Tommo jokes, resembles an illustrated edition of Oliver Goldsmith's *History of the Earth, and Animated Nature.*

The natives make significant use of facial tattoos, which function as legible signs allowing Tommo to begin interpreting their character. The tattoos enhance the signifying power of the face and help Tommo read what he first found illegible. Mehevi is adorned with broad stripes forming a triangle across his face. Tommo recognizes a correlation between Mehevi's facial tattoo and his physical stature. In Mehevi, nature and artifice have come together. His magisterial body identifies him as a noble savage; his tattoos confirm his status.

Kory-Kory, alternatively, has been tattooed "with a view of improving the handiwork of nature, and perhaps prompted by a desire to add to the engaging expression of his countenance." Displaying "three broad longitudinal stripes of tattooing," his face reminds Tommo "of those unhappy wretches whom I have sometimes observed gazing out sentimentally from behind the grated bars of a prison window" (*W*, I, p. 83). (During his American travels Melville may have visited Auburn Prison, the largest tourist destination in western New York after Niagara Falls.) Identifying a resemblance between Kory-Kory's facial tattoos and prison bars, Tommo implies that any tattoo or, for that matter, any physical adornment functions as a kind of prison.

Introducing the characters he encounters, Tommo typically notices their facial appearances. None intrigue him more than Fayaway. He describes her complexion, olive yet not so olive to mask her blushes. He dwells upon her mouth: her full lips, dazzling teeth, playful smile. Fayaway's beauty is magical: she seems all things to all men. Tommo does not stop his description of Fayaway at her face. He also titillates his readers with suggestive comments about her body. When she stoops, her long, dark brown hair hides "her lovely bosom" from view. Melville cleverly implies that when she is not stooping, which is most of the time, then nothing hides her lovely bosom from view. The table of contents calls her provocative behavior while canoeing a "beautiful freak" (*W*, I, pp. 86, xi). With an exclamation of delight, she stands erect in the canoe, slips the mantle from her shoulders, extends her arms, and spreads her garment like a sail. Her lithe, naked body forms the mast. Sigmund Freud had one disturbed patient who read the whipping scenes in *Uncle Tom's Cabin* for purposes of "pleasurable auto-erotic satisfaction." Among nineteenth-century readers, *Typee* ranked above all other works of literature for purposes of onanistic gratification.

Fayaway's voluptuous body adds allure to the narrative, but her face may be more important to the theme of cultural difference between the Westerner and the South Pacific islander. When she is in a contemplative mood, her eyes seem "placid yet unfathomable." Illuminated by emotion, they beam "upon the beholder like stars" (*W*, I, p. 86). Tommo's capacity to read her face suggests that he has partly developed his ability to understand the natives using physiognomy. Sometimes he can read her thoughts; other times he cannot. The legibility of her face depends upon her mood.

Tommo's ability to understand the Typee natives apparently improves over the course of the narrative. At one point, several of them issue a collective warning, all glancing sternly toward him. After the incident, he observes: "The lively countenances of these people are wonderfully indicative of the emotions of the soul, and the imperfections of their oral language are more than compensated for by the nervous eloquence of their looks and gestures. I could plainly trace, in every varying expression of their faces, all those passions which had been thus unexpectedly aroused in their bosoms" (*W*, I, p. 142). Tommo seems to have mastered the ability to read the natives, but he has not secured their confidence. On this occasion, their stern glances caution him against speaking with Marnoo, a tabbooed wanderer who might be able to get him off the island.

Once Toby has escaped from the valley never to return, Tommo is in a precarious state. Unless he can gain the confidence of the Typee, he has no hope of escaping. After they warn him away from Marnoo, he devises a new plan. He decides to feign confidence in them. It may take time, but he hopes to convince them that he has reconciled himself to life in Typee by assuming a pleasant demeanor to allay their suspicions, revive their confidence, and relax their watchfulness, allowing him to take advantage of whatever opportunity for escape that may present itself.

As part of his plan, Tommo makes some popguns for the children. Such is the gun's allure that soon almost everyone in the community, young and old, wants a popgun. Tommo obliges. The episode introduces another similarity between *Typee* and *Paradise Lost*. Satan invents firearms in Book 6 of *Paradise Lost*; Tommo makes popguns in Chapter 19 of *Typee*. In other words, both Satan and Tommo are responsible for bringing guns into paradise. The popgun episode further parallels Tommo with the missionaries. Despite his animosity toward them, he, too, is complicit in the Westernization of the South Pacific islanders. He introduces Western technology to Typee.

From his own perspective, Tommo's plan to win the confidence of the Typee natives seems to be working. From their perspective, he will not win them over until he lets them tattoo his face. Only then will they accept him as a member of the community. Understandably Tommo refuses to take this ultimate step. The tattoo would effectively prevent him from returning to Western society. Tommo puns: "I now felt convinced that in some luckless hour I should be disfigured in such a manner as never more to have the *face* to return to my countrymen, even should an opportunity offer" (*W*, I, p. 219).

Karky, the local tattoo artist, sees Tommo's face as an unparalleled opportunity to practice his craft and chases after him brandishing a pointy shark's tooth and various other tattooing implements. Tommo partly acquiesces and agrees to let him tattoo his arms. Karky insists that the face must be tattooed first. Tommo explains: "I was fairly driven to despair; nothing but the utter ruin of my 'face divine,' as the poets call it, would, I perceived, satisfy the inexorable Mehevi and his chiefs, or rather, that infernal Karky, for he was at the bottom of it all" (*W*, I, p. 220).

Tommo's words echo *Paradise Lost*, which gave currency to the phrase, "the human face divine." After Milton, numerous other poets repeated the phrase to emphasize the godlike image of man's countenance. In his translation of Homer's *Iliad*, for example, Alexander Pope refers to Hector's "Face divine." Perhaps most important in terms of Melville's influences is the English translation of *The Lusiad*, the epic by the Portuguese poet, Luís de Camões. In this poem, Vasco da Gama and his men, who have been "Taught to behold the rays of godhead shine, / Fair imaged in the human face divine," are horrified by the monstrous faces of the pagan idols they encounter in India.[4] The Miltonic concept of "the human face divine" gave Melville an idea which would pervade his oeuvre.

Despite its suitability, Melville's use of the phrase offers a good example of why readers were skeptical of *Typee* when it first appeared. Men who sailed before the mast were not generally known for their ability to dash off lines from *Paradise Lost*. Grace Greenwood, to name one of the most astute contemporary readers, parodied Melville's use of the Miltonic phrase in her spoof of *Typee*. Speaking as Melville, she described a verse recital of a native bard whose poetic inspiration shines through his "tattooed visage like the light of a candle through a half-ripe pumpkin, carved by infant sculptors, in the form of 'the human face divine'" (*CR*, p. 76).

Chapter 31, which follows the one in which Tommo despairs over the possible ruin of his face, is structured differently from the other chapters. It consists of six short sections, each addressing a distinct subtopic about life in Typee and all separated by lines of asterisks. At first glance, this chapter seems little more than a place for Melville to put the extra tidbits of information he could not conveniently fit anywhere else. This miscellaneous chapter significantly alters the narrative pace, however. As Tommo had adjusted himself to a potentially lengthy stay in Typee over the previous half dozen or so chapters, the pace of the book had slowed to reflect his languorous existence. Quickening the narrative in preparation for the story's denouement, Chapter 31 anticipates a cinematic montage sequence in terms of its purpose as well as its structure.

In the following chapter, Tommo becomes aware of a threat more insidious than tattooing as he briefly glimpses a native collection of shrunken heads, one being a white man's. Coming after the idyllic passages preceding it, this startling sight reminds him of the threat of cannibalism, which he had been neglecting. In his review of *Typee*, Nathaniel Hawthorne noted the shift with humor and hyperbole: "On one page, we read of manners and modes of life that indicate a whole system of innocence and peace; and on the next, we catch a glimpse of a smoked human head, and the half-picked skeleton of what had been (in a culinary sense) a *well-dressed* man" (*CR*, p. 22). Seeing these heads, Tommo fears for his own. He is shocked at the thought that the people he had been attempting to ingratiate could turn on him and wish him harm. There's no time for dawdling. Tommo must get off the island as quickly as possible.

The opportunity to escape occurs as an Australian whaler enters the bay seeking to replenish its crew. Some Typee natives agree to let Tommo go while others want to detain him further. Marheyo wishes him well. Tommo explains, "I shall never forget the benevolent expression of his countenance. He placed his arm upon my shoulder, and emphatically pronounced the only two English words I had taught him – 'Home' and 'Mother'" (*W*, I, p. 248). But Marheyo's sympathetic countenance is not the last native visage Tommo sees as he leaves the island. The last one he sees is Mow-Mow's hideously tattooed face, deformed by the loss of an eye and made even more menacing by a battle scar received at the hands of a spear-wielding enemy. Melville added the character of Mow-Mow late in the composition of *Typee* to enhance the drama of the closing sequence. As Tommo sails from the shore in an open boat, Mow-Mow swims after him, a tomahawk clenched between his teeth. When Mow-Mow gets within reach, Tommo takes a boat hook and dashes it into Mow-Mow's throat, forcing him underwater. Tommo looks back to see him rise to the surface. The sight of Mow-Mow's face sticks in his memory: "Never shall I forget the ferocious expression of his countenance" (*W*, I, p. 252).

Seeing Mow-Mow clearly, Tommo penetrates his countenance and, for the first time, is able to read the native face to see what the Typee really think of him. Mow-Mow cares for neither the technology nor the ideas he has brought them. Tommo may have felt like he was ingratiating himself to the Typee natives, but Mow-Mow's menacing visage lets Tommo know that he had never gained their confidence. Or, to use a phrase of more recent currency, he never won over the hearts and minds of the Typee. Only upon his departure does he realize the deep animosity the natives feel toward him. As Tommo, the American, leaves this foreign land behind, the last thing he sees is the angry face of the native.

Omoo: the rover as flaneur

Defending *Omoo* against some harsh criticism, Evert Duyckinck found absurd how one critic judged the book's narrator according to the conduct of civilized society, "as if a vagabond, *in a book*, in a barbarous tropical island, was to be measured by the same standard as a polite *flaneur* on the Boulevards or Regent Street" (*CR*, p. 189). Duyckinck was more prescient than he realized. Though he refused to compare Melville's narrator with the sophisticated urban observer known as the flaneur, perhaps that is precisely how the narrator *should* be seen. Pitching the book to John Murray, Melville himself explained that *Omoo* depicted "the 'man about town' sort of life, led, at the present day, by roving sailors in the Pacific" (*W*, XIV, p. 78). Furthermore, much of the humor in this very funny book comes from the way its narrator ironically assumes an air of urbane sophistication to comment on what he sees while island hopping through the South Pacific.

Omoo resumes the story of Melville's personal adventures where *Typee* leaves off. At the end of *Typee* Tommo is rescued by an Australian whaler; at the beginning of *Omoo* the narrator finds himself aboard the *Julia*, an Australian whaler. Otherwise there is little connection between the two books. It is unnecessary to have read *Typee* to understand what's happening in *Omoo*. The name Tommo is not reused either. Early in *Omoo*, the narrator says that his shipmates aboard the *Julia* called him Typee. On the "round robin," the document the rebellious crew members sign, the narrator signs himself Typee. Among the Hawthornes, Melville was known as both Mr Typee and Mr Omoo. Calling the narrator either adds unnecessary confusion. It is easiest to call him Melville – always assuming a distinction between Melville the author and Melville the narrator.

Like the urban flaneur, the narrator of *Omoo* does a lot of walking and looking, but he does so along the byways of the South-Sea islands. In his preface, he calls himself "a roving sailor" who had spent three months in Tahiti and Imeeo "under circumstances most favorable for correct observations on the social condition of the natives." Describing his activities as roving and observing, he comes close to identifying with the flaneur. The preface contains other comments elaborating the role he assumes. He calls himself "an unbiased observer" and tells his readers that *Omoo* – the unusual-sounding word he has chosen for his title – comes from the dialect of the Marquesas Islands and means "a rover, or rather, a person wandering from one island to another" (*W*, II, p. xiv).

When talking about *Omoo*, modern commentators often use the terms "rover" and "beachcomber" interchangeably. In *Omoo* Melville *never* uses "beachcomber" to describe himself. Defining the word, he notes: "This is a term much in vogue among sailors in the Pacific. It is applied to certain roving characters, who, without attaching themselves permanently to any vessel, ship now and then for a short cruise in a whaler; but upon the condition only of being honorably discharged the very next time the anchor takes hold of the bottom; no matter where. They are," he continues, "a reckless, rollicking set, wedded to the Pacific, and never dreaming of ever doubling Cape Horn again on a homeward-bound passage. Hence, their reputation is a bad one" (*W*, II, p. 81). This note clarifies that the word "beachcomber" applies to "certain roving sailors," not all roving sailors. Recognizing the limitations of the term yet reluctant to abandon it, one modern reader coined the oxymoron "gentleman-beachcomber" to characterize Tommo's perspective in *Typee*.[5] The concept of a gentleman-beachcomber approaches what Melville meant by calling his character a rover in *Omoo*.

The beachcomber, as Melville's definition suggests, has turned his back on Western civilization. The rover, as the narrator's behavior in *Omoo* suggests, tries to maintain some conventions of and connections to civilized society. The beachcomber is generally illiterate; the rover knows how to read and write. The beachcomber is guided by his physical urges: he wanders wherever he can find food, shelter, drink, or sex. The rover is guided by his intellect: he wanders in search of objects and ideas to provoke contemplation. The beachcomber lives a hand-to-mouth existence; the rover lives an eye-to-brain existence.

The differences between the beachcomber and the rover also point to a distinction between *Typee* and *Omoo*. Herman Melville called *Omoo* "a fitting successor to *Typee*." Whereas his first book depicts Polynesian life in its primitive state, the second shows it "as affected by intercourse with the whites" (*W*, XIV, p. 78). *Typee* opposes whites and Polynesians. Though Tommo critiques the missionaries, he ultimately must choose between native culture and Western society. Escaping Typee valley, he returns to the missionaries' side. *Omoo* is more complex. As Charles Olson observed, *Typee* is Melville's "Song of innocence"; *Omoo* is his "Song of experience."[6] Portraying Polynesian life as influenced by Western society, Melville not only shows natives who have been corrupted and Christianized by the visiting missionaries, he also depicts sailors who have abandoned the commercial vessels that symbolize Western culture in favor of an uncertain existence on the fringes of society. The beachcomber has passed the point of no return; the rover hugs that point yet stays this side of it. Balancing here requires a steady vigil. If the rover is not careful, he could slip into beachcombery.

The rover's ability to read, both literally and figuratively, helps him maintain his precarious position. The Polynesian natives Melville encounters distinguish him from the beachcombers and associate him with the missionaries because of his literacy. One native who has converted to Christianity calls him a "mickonaree," meaning "a man able to read, and cunning in the use of the pen" (*W*, II, p. 164). Like the flaneur, the rover's literacy extends beyond the ability to read written texts to the ability to read the local terrain. Much as Tommo tries to read the native faces in *Typee*, Melville reads the face of the country in *Omoo*. Observing the landscape to understand national character resembles the task of interpreting facial features to understand personality. To the flaneur, Walter Benjamin observed, "everything is face."[7]

Dependent upon whatever happens to catch his eye, the flaneur's reflections have a fundamentally random nature. So do Melville's in *Omoo*. In his preface, he emphasizes the random, unsystematic nature of his personal observations: "In no respect does the author make pretensions to philosophic research. In a familiar way, he has merely described what he has seen; and if reflections are occasionally indulged in, they are spontaneous, and such as would, very probably, suggest themselves to the most casual observer" (*W*, II, p. xv). This random quality piqued some contemporary readers. J. A. Heraud, for one, said that because Melville's observations "follow in arbitrary succession," they do not sustain "any connected interest." It is easy to dismiss Heraud's comments – Thomas Carlyle called him "a loquacious scribacious little man" – but he makes an important point by emphasizing the random quality of Melville's observations. Despite its apparent randomness, *Omoo* is a well paced and finely balanced narrative. Sergei Eisenstein, for one, thought it admirably constructed.[8]

During the book's early chapters, Melville defines himself through comparison, that is, by describing his shipmates aboard the *Julia* and revealing his relationship with them. His closest friend is Dr Long Ghost. Well educated, the doctor quotes Virgil, talks of Hobbes, and repeats *Hudibras* by the canto. Having originally signed on as ship's physician, the doctor quit his post after a fight with the captain and moved into the forecastle with the common sailors. Befriending the doctor, Melville associates with a well-read man of leisure, and takes on similar characteristics himself, which help him assume the role of South-Seas flaneur.

Nearing Tahiti, the crew, upset with the way the *Julia* is being managed, refuses all further duty. Consequently, they are taken ashore in leg irons, a condition that hardly allows the flaneur to engage in one of his defining behaviors. The chains do not prevent Melville from enjoying the flaneur's other characteristic behavior. He sees the village of Papeetee with a keen eye. Once ashore, he and his fellow crew members are handed over to their native gaoler, Captain Bob, a genial fellow who only locks them up in the Calabooza at night. They are free to roam during the day. Such freedoms give Melville much opportunity for seeing Tahiti and reflecting on what he sees.

Other contemporary readers saw similarities between the observations Herman Melville made in his early writings and the observations of the urban flaneur. After reading *Typee*, Henry David Thoreau found Tommo's observations about daily life among the islanders similar to the kinds of observations that could be made while promenading down Broadway.[9] But Tommo's comments in *Typee* emanate from a static perspective. The true flaneur needs a Broadway or the boulevards to structure his observations.

Omoo has Broom Road. The name of the road comes from the fact that convicts maintain its surface by sweeping it clean. Broom Road encircles a good part of Tahiti and offers a place for Melville's narrator to walk and a way for him to organize his thoughts. It's no Regent Street, but it does give him the opportunity to engage in similar activities as those who stroll more renowned avenues. Though he walks along Broom Road for miles and miles, he never tires of "the continual change of scenery." His promenades mimic the leisurely pace of the urban flaneur. In *Omoo*, the word "stroll" occurs frequently. Melville takes "a pleasant little stroll down the Broom Road" one day and "a pensive stroll" on another. Late in the story, he celebrates the activity of walking over other means of locomotion: "Say what they will of the glowing independence one feels in the saddle, give me the first morning flush of your cheery pedestrian!" (*W*, II, pp. 115, 141, 295, 253).

An evening stroll allows him to see the missionaries and their families. The sight of them reminds him of home and makes him long for "a dress coat and beaver, that I might step up and pay my respects." Instead of a beaver hat, he wears a makeshift turban fashioned from a calico sailor's frock, its sleeves dangling down the back of his neck. His headgear prompts Dr Long Ghost to call him the "Bashaw with Two Tails" (*W*, II, pp. 167, 236). The doctor's epithet indicates Melville's liminal status. While he assumes that he can mingle with the missionaries socially, his outlandish headgear suggests that he belongs to a different society altogether.

Unaware that some Westerners might be put off by his appearance, he approaches an old missionary woman and a pretty girl with blond ringlets to wish them a pleasant evening. As this tanned and turbanned young man approaches these two, the younger one screams, and the older one nearly faints. Shocked by their reaction, he retreats to the safety of the Calabooza. So far, he had been imagining that he could still mingle in polite society, but this encounter reveals to him that he has lost his cultural moorings. The realization disturbs him to such an extent that he prefers the safety of confinement over the freedom of Broom Road.

In other contemporary American literature – Edgar Allan Poe's "The Man of the Crowd" comes to mind – the flaneur's sophisticated mode of observing is often contrasted with the unsophisticated badaud or gawker. In *Omoo*, Melville also describes other, less sophisticated ways of seeing. During his peregrinations, he happens to enter a church where he sees a strange looking native man: "He wore nothing but a coarse, scant mantle, of faded tappa; and from his staring, bewildered manner, I set him down as an aged bumpkin from the interior, unaccustomed to the strange sights and sounds of the metropolis" (*W*, II, p. 171). This bumpkin plays badaud to Melville's flaneur. The old man merely gawks in amazement whereas Melville looks, penetrating the surface of what he sees in order to understand its deeper meaning. Incorporating a native badaud within his personal narrative, Melville assumes an air of superiority, which reinforces the idea that his roots remain in the flaneur's domain, the realm of Western civilization.

Over the course of their imprisonment, the status of the prisoners becomes increasingly uncertain. The longer they stay, the more freedom they have. The more they roam around Tahiti, the more anxious the Tahitians are to see them leave. Eventually, the men drift from the Calabooza and go their own ways. Melville and Dr Long Ghost sail to Imeeo, a neighboring island where they meet Zeke and Shorty, a pair of comical farmers who take them on as farmhands. Melville and the doctor find farming far more work than they had imagined and hang up their hoes to explore other parts of Imeeo.

Their wanderings take them around the island, but when they reach the settlement of Partoowye, Melville has the opportunity to use his flaneur-like abilities the way they were meant to be used, that is, in the observation of a city. Partoowye is no Paris, but the main street that runs through it "is broad, and serpentine; well shaded, from one end to the other; and as pretty a place for a morning promenade, as any lounger could wish" (*W*, II, p. 284). Like Tahiti's Broom Road, Partoowye's broad avenue provides a road that structures Melville's observations in *Omoo*.

Being the closest thing Imeeo has to a city, Partoowye lets him parody urban American social customs. As Melville and Dr Long Ghost stroll the principal avenue one morning, they make several social calls. Melville observes that "the hour could not have been the fashionable one in Partoowye; since the ladies were invariably in dishabille" (*W*, II, p. 285). Subsequent American authors – Stephen Crane in *The Monster*, Kate Chopin in *The Awakening* – would sharply critique the formality and artificiality of the formal social call; Melville's satire has a softer tone and bawdier implications: Women need not dress for their callers in a place where nakedness is the norm.

The most astonishing thing they see on their stroll is a block of two-story, Western-style frame houses fast falling into decay. Curious to know who could have been trying to improve the value of real estate in Partoowye, they make some inquiries and learn that "the block had been thrown up by a veritable Yankee (one might have known that), a house carpenter by trade, and a bold, enterprising fellow by nature" (*W*, II, p. 285). Melville's description echoes Washington Irving's "Rip Van Winkle." Upon returning to town after his long absence, Rip discovers that his favorite haunt, the village inn, has been replaced by a "large, ricketty wooden building . . . with great gaping windows, some of them broken, and mended with old hats and petticoats, and over the door was printed, 'The Union Hotel, by Jonathan Doolittle.'"

Falling asleep in the British colonies and waking up in the United States, Rip Van Winkle sees the dark side of American culture. A nation that encourages both thriftiness and the entrepreneurial spirit can sometimes encourage people to work too quickly, cut corners, and use shoddy building materials. Seeing the frame houses of Partoowye in relation to his knowledge of native South Pacific culture, Melville also makes the quickly constructed frame house symbolic of the United States, but he goes further than Irving does. Two-story frame houses created in the South Pacific, like the futile endeavors of the missionaries, reveal how ludicrous efforts to impose American culture onto different parts of the world can be.

Partoowye Melville based on Fa-re, a different settlement on a different island which the prominent British missionary William Ellis described in *Polynesian*

Researches. Relying heavily on Ellis for much of the details in the second half of *Omoo*, Melville integrated the material so seamlessly that his reliance on this source went unnoticed for nearly a century. Melville's expert ability to use his sources stems from his own flaneur-like capacity. For him, reading another's book of travels was almost like strolling through the places it describes. St Loe Strachey recognized the importance of Melville's source material even as he emphasized his originality. To make his point, Strachey found a walking metaphor appropriate: "Melville in his prose was not an imitator. He was always a most original man. When, however, he took his walks abroad, whether in ancient or in modern literature, quantities of the paint on the gates he passed through came off on his clothes."[10]

Melville himself acknowledged the value of source material in the development of his own writing. "Our best and surest road to knowledge," said Lord Kames in a passage Melville scored in his copy of Isaac Disraeli's *The Literary Character; or, The History of Men of Genius*, "is by profiting from the labours of others, and making their experience our own."[11] Lord Kames's words can be paraphrased to suit Melville's reliance on Ellis. Melville benefitted from reading *Polynesian Researches* yet made Ellis's experiences his own. Reading provoked Melville's imagination and allowed him to make poignant observations based on written sources that are remarkably consistent with those based on his own travels.

Readers who supported missionary work in the South Seas were disturbed by what Melville had to say in *Omoo*, but those who appreciated a good yarn found much to enjoy. For the most part, *Omoo* was warmly received by nineteenth-century readers, a group that included that sprightly man of arts and letters, Edward Lear.[12] Given his skills as landscape painter, travel writer, and humorist, Lear could find much to appreciate in *Omoo*. As a rover, Melville carefully scrutinizes the landscape of the South Pacific during his peregrinations, describing whatever happens to come under his gaze with wit and charm.

Becoming a great writer: *Mardi, Redburn, White-Jacket*

While working on *Mardi*, Melville suddenly realized he was a great writer. Since completing *Typee*, he knew he had talent, but with his third book he reached a deeper understanding of what he could do with his pen. Two important aspects of his literary life facilitated this personal epiphany. Whereas his previous books had been loosely based on his own real-life adventures, *Mardi* was pure fiction. As Melville gave his imagination free rein for the first time, he saw how fast and how far it could run. Furthermore, he had ample reading opportunities during the composition of *Mardi* and took full advantage of them, immersing himself in the literature of great writers from the past. Not only did these authors significantly influence his style, they also gave him a basis for comparison. As *Mardi* developed, he recognized that his own writing did not fall very short of his models from literary history. He continued experimenting throughout the book, testing his talent to see where it could take him. The result can be characterized as a literary extravaganza or, in the words of the pun-loving Oakey Hall, "a regular Mardi-gras of a novel" (*CR*, p. 225).

Many contemporary readers disliked the self-indulgence *Mardi* exemplified. Melville realized that the only way he could hope to sell books and support his family with his pen would be to impose limits on both his imagination and his expression. With *Redburn* and *White-Jacket*, he returned to real-life adventure for inspiration. He saw this step as a retrograde movement. After the intellectual and imaginative leaps he had made in *Mardi*, he was returning to the same method he had used with his first two books. But *Redburn* and *White-Jacket* reflect his growing literary maturity. *Mardi* showed Melville what his boundless imagination could do; his next two books provided realistic boundaries within which he could exercise his imagination. Writing *Mardi*, he had lost control of his narrative; *Redburn* and *White-Jacket* restored his narrative control. The three books show him cultivating the literary genius he would bring to his finest works over the next few years.

The difference between *Mardi* and Melville's two previous books is notable from the start. The ingratiating tone of his earlier prefaces has disappeared. In the preface to *Mardi*, as Willard Thorp suggested, Melville wears "a slightly malicious smile."[13] The preface consists of only two sentences, one long and one short. Since some considered his previous books romances, Melville told readers that this time he had written a romance to see if it would be read as truth. Brief as it is, the preface embodies the irritation Melville felt toward contemporary readers, most of whom wanted to know what they would be reading before they read it. They preferred books that fell into neat, recognizable categories. He refused to let his readers off so easily. Breaking the conventions of accepted literary genres and challenging his readers' expectations, Melville dared to make them think.

Melville incorporated several different modes of discourse in *Mardi*. His shift from adventure tale to romantic interlude to travelogue-satire partly reflects his shifting intentions as he composed the work. As John Evelev observed, Melville's attitude toward professional authorship changed during the book's composition. He began *Mardi* by writing in the manner of Washington Irving, that is, with an air of aristocratic indolence. In the middle, allegorical part, Melville assumed the voice of the reformer. Becoming more self-reflexive as the story approaches its conclusion, he took on the aura of the professional artist who writes for the ages.[14]

Mardi deliberately flaunts the author's literary knowledge. Its literary references achieve a level of sophistication unequaled in either of his previous works. *Mardi* can be read as a record of Melville's reading from mid-1847 through 1848. During the book's composition, his mind was in a malleable state. He could scarcely read any text without it leaving its impress on his mind and his work. A great sense of fun pervades Melville's literary references and allusions in *Mardi*, too. Immersed in the world of books, he thoroughly enjoyed himself. For example, his first-person narrator, who would assume the name of Taji as the story progressed, laments the unlettered life of the sailor in the opening chapter, "Foot in Stirrup." To his chagrin, no one else aboard his vessel shares an interest in literature or philosophy. Growing weary of traditional tales and ballads, Taji longs for someone who could quote "from Burton on Blue Devils" (*W*, III, p. 5).

Melville had only read Robert Burton's *Anatomy of Melancholy* after returning from his lengthy sea voyage, but he makes Taji aware of the work before he sails. A reference to Sir Thomas Browne – another author Melville read while writing *Mardi* – soon follows. Throughout its text, *Mardi* shows the influence of Browne's characteristic style – his use of paradoxical aphorisms, his conjoined word pairs, his ability to sustain a rhythm in prose that approaches verse.[15] François Rabelais is another author Melville read during the composition of *Mardi* whose influence its text clearly reveals.

Taji feels such close camaraderie with books that their authors seem like old friends to him. Describing his shipmate Jarl, a superstitious, yet practical-minded Skyeman, Taji compares him to "my Right Reverend friend, Bishop Berkeley – truly, one of your lords spiritual – who, metaphysically speaking, holding all objects to be mere optical delusions, was, notwithstanding, extremely matter-of-fact in all matters touching matter itself." Taji's words reflect the sense of ease Melville was developing. Complex philosophical notions that might stymie less accomplished authors, Melville tosses off with humor and aplomb. Taji feels friendly toward other important figures in literary history stretching back as far as ancient Greece. Thucydides he calls "my Peloponnesian friend" (*W*, III, pp. 63, 104). Taji's experience is Melville's. It is also that of anyone who reads deeply and thoughtfully. Reading turns authors into friends and readers into time travelers.

The biographical nature of *Redburn* presented Melville with a challenge. He wanted to continue the same kinds of literary references he had used in *Mardi*, but he knew that it would be inappropriate to endow the teenaged Wellingborough Redburn with a preternatural knowledge of books and authors. His literary references in *Redburn* reveal how an indulgence in *Mardi* became controlled and channeled within the framework of his next book. Melville made numerous literary references in *Redburn*, but intentionally restricted himself to books which someone of Redburn's youth and experience could have read. The books Redburn knows are ones he has encountered in his father's library.

The literary allusions in *Redburn* provide an example of how the limits Melville imposed upon himself actually allowed him to enhance the complexity of his narrative. Redburn's knowledge of books is inextricably linked to the memories of his father. As the story of Redburn's youthful voyage to Liverpool unfolds, the motif of the book gradually becomes a powerful symbol for the father. In the "old family Plutarch," for example, Redburn remembers reading about "severe and chastising fathers, fathers whose sense of duty overcomes the sense of love, and who every day, in some sort, play the part of Brutus, who ordered his son away to execution" (*W*, IV, p. 67). Melville's use of irony works well. Indebted to his father for his books, Redburn reads in them about fathers whose moral sense leads to their sons' destruction.

Among the numerous books in his father's library, none have influenced Redburn more than the collection of European and English travel guides. As a child, Redburn had never tired of staring at the strange title pages, which resemble "the mustached faces of foreigners" (*W*, IV, p. 141). This resemblance presents another example of Melville's personification of books. It also reinforces the importance he attributed to a book's front matter. The front of a book is like a person's face: it introduces the reader to the work and provides a general indication of the whole.

Redburn takes his father's Liverpool guidebook with him once he signs aboard the *Highlander*. Some of the most delightful moments in *Redburn* involve the difficulties Melville's title character experiences as he tries to find his way around Liverpool using this antiquated guidebook. Though his father and his father's books have exerted a crucial influence on his young life, Redburn ultimately must leave them behind him. "The thing that had guided the father," he concludes, "could not guide the son" (*W*, IV, p. 157). Redburn's personal growth parallels Melville's literary maturation. Marked by its modernity, his description of Liverpool reads nothing like an old guidebook. As Newton Arvin observed, Herman Melville's Liverpool looks forward to James Joyce's Dublin.[16]

Though the fictional world Melville created in *Mardi* gave his imagination the opportunity to flourish, paradoxically it hindered one particular aspect of his writing. *Mardi* let him imagine whatever he wished, but Melville was often at his best when he used real-world detail as a jumping-off point for his flights of fancy. The realistic settings of *Redburn* and *White-Jacket* tether his imagination and prevent it from getting out of control. But he appreciated realistic detail for its own sake as well. His fascination with contemporary material culture partly stemmed from his ability to recognize the philosophical ramifications of the everyday. But material objects fascinated him in and of themselves, too. He could see far enough into the future to know that the experiences of the nineteenth-century sailor aboard a merchant vessel or a man-of-war would be lost unless someone like him recorded them. This documentary aspect of Melville's work often disappears in the shadow of his titanic imagination, but it is there nonetheless.

In its numerous details of life aboard a merchant vessel, *Redburn* manifests Melville's desire to capture the ephemeral. *White-Jacket* makes that intention explicit. White Jacket – both the title of the book and the name of the first-person narrator come from the pale grego he wears – decides to "jot down in our memories a few little things pertaining to our man-of-war world." Justifying his decision, he explains, "I let nothing slip, however small; and feel myself actuated by the same motive which has prompted many worthy old chroniclers, to set down the merest trifles concerning things that are des-tined to pass away entirely from the earth, and which, if not preserved in the nick of time, must infallibly perish from the memories of man" (*W*, V, p. 282).

Incorporating numerous sailor proverbs in *Redburn* and *White-Jacket*, Melville exercised his desire to capture the ephemeral. Unlike Edgar Allan Poe, who disdained proverbs, Melville recognized the importance of getting these traditional sayings down on paper before they disappeared. Many of the sailor sayings included in *Redburn* and *White-Jacket* are not recorded elsewhere. If Melville had not captured them, they would indeed be lost.[17]

White-Jacket brings together Melville's bookish references and his interest in traditional oral culture. While incorporating many literary comments, Chapter 41, "A Man-of-War Library," also conveys the limitations of book learning. In a large cask aboard the *Neversink*, White Jacket discovers "numer-ous invaluable but unreadable tomes, that might have been purchased cheap at the auction of some college-professor's library." The books include a copy of "Blair's Lectures, University Edition." The work Melville had in mind was Hugh Blair's *Lectures on Rhetoric and Belles Lettres*, specifically, the edition annotated by Abraham Mills, first published at Philadelphia in 1833, and designated on its spine as the "University Edition." Blair's *Lectures* gave its readers a thorough grounding in criticism, rhetoric, and English language and literature. Though "a fine treatise on rhetoric," White Jacket observes, it has "nothing to say about nautical phrases, such as *splicing the main-brace, passing a gammoning, puddinging the dolphin*, and *making a Carrick-bend*" (*W*, V, p. 168). Melville clearly understood an important truth: There is more to language and literature than is dreamt of by linguists and rhetoricians.

Melville's impulse to capture the ephemeral parallels his desire to record passing thoughts as they occur. *Mardi*, *Redburn*, and *White-Jacket* manifest his characteristic thought processes. In all three books, the quotidian forms the basis for wide-ranging philosophical reflections. Melville's imagination bridged the everyday and the eternal. A simple fact conjures up an association in his mind, which leads to a series of provocative ideas and images that take him far afield. So far does he go, so deep does he dive that he often ends up plumbing the depths of the soul.

One of the finest passages in *Mardi* occurs in Chapter 32, "Xiphius Platypterius." The chapter title comes from the Latin name for swordfish. It would seem to indicate an essay on natural history, but over its course it becomes something else entirely. The following extract begins with Melville's personification of the swordfish:

> A right valiant and jaunty Chevalier is our hero; going about with his long Toledo perpetually drawn. Rely upon it, he will fight you to the hilt, for his bony blade has never a scabbard. He himself sprang from it at birth; yea, at the very moment he leaped into the Battle of Life; as we mortals ourselves spring all naked and scabbardless into the world. Yet, rather, are we scabbards to our souls. And the drawn soul of genius is more glittering than the drawn cimeter of Saladin. But how many let their steel sleep, till it eat up the scabbard itself, and both corrode to rust-chips. Saw you ever the hillocks of old Spanish anchors, and anchor-stocks of ancient galleons, at the bottom of Callao Bay? The world is full of old Tower armories, and dilapidated Venetian arsenals, and rusty old rapiers. But true warriors polish their good blades by the bright beams of the morning; and gird them on to their brave sirloins; and watch for rust spots as for foes; and by many stout thrusts and stoccadoes keep their metal lustrous and keen, as the spears of the Northern Lights charging over Greenland.   (*W*, III, p. 104)

Starting with his personification of the swordfish as a saber-wielding chevalier, Taji realizes that his figure of speech is inadequate: the swordfish has no scabbard. This realization elicits a number of imaginative associations. Surely all swords have scabbards. The swordfish's scabbard can only be the body of the mother who gave birth to him. He then generalizes his metaphor to suit mankind. Man, too, is born without a scabbard. Reiterating the body-as-scabbard idea, he likens man's soul to his sword, associates soul with genius, and laments how many people let their genius rust in their scabbards, undrawn, unpolished, unused. The figurative use of rust conjures up other literal images of rust. The passage suggests how true warriors or true geniuses use and care for their swords and ends with an extraordinary simile comparing the sword to the aurora borealis.

Redburn and *White-Jacket* contain passages of linked analogies that are similarly structured but homier in their beginnings and less extravagant in their imaginative leaps. In Chapter 7, "Breakfast, Dinner, and Supper," for example, White Jacket reflects on the proper time for dining. After describing the noon hour at length and emphasizing its importance over other dinner hours, he develops an extended personification of the sun as a hill-climbing traveler who pauses at his peak to dine. He then reflects on the meaning of the word "afternoon" and conjures up further associations:

> The rest of the day is called *afternoon*; the very sound of which fine old Saxon word conveys a feeling of the lee bulwarks and a nap; a summer sea – soft breezes creeping over it; dreamy dolphins gliding in the distance. *Afternoon!* the word implies, that it is an after-piece, coming after the grand drama of the day; something to be taken leisurely and lazily. But how can this be, if you dine at five? For, after all, though *Paradise Lost* be a noble poem, and we men-of-war's men, no doubt, largely partake in the immortality of the immortals; yet, let us candidly confess it, shipmates, that, upon the whole, our dinners are the most momentous affairs of these lives we lead beneath the moon. What were a day without a dinner? a dinnerless day! such a day had better be a night.   (*W*, V, pp. 28–29)

Though the texts of *Redburn* and *White-Jacket* prove that Melville could indulge in similar kinds of philosophical reflections as he had in *Mardi* without losing his narrative thread or his reader's attention, something did get lost when he shifted from the extravagance of *Mardi* to the more controlled subjects of *Redburn* and *White-Jacket*. No part of *Mardi* better illustrates this than Chapter 119, "Dreams." As one of Melville's most appreciative contemporary reviewers commented, "We have small respect for authors who are wilful, and cannot be advised; but we reverence a man when God's *must* is upon him, and he does his work in his own and other's spite. Portions of *Mardi* are written with this divine impulse, and they thrill through every fibre of the reader with an electric force. The chapter on dreams is an example" (*CR*, p. 239).

Taji is speaking, but there can be little doubt that what he articulates reflects Melville's own ambitious literary dreams:

Like a grand, ground swell, Homer's old organ rolls its vast volumes
under the light frothy wave-crests of Anacreon and Hafiz; and high over
my ocean, sweet Shakespeare soars, like all the larks of the spring.
Throned on my sea-side, like Canute, bearded Ossian smites his hoar
harp, wreathed with wild-flowers, in which warble my Wallers; blind
Milton sings bass to my Petrarchs and Priors, and laureats crown me
with bays.

In me, many worthies recline, and converse. I list to St. Paul who
argues the doubts of Montaigne; Julian the Apostate cross-questions
Augustine; and Thomas-a-Kempis unrolls his old black letters for all to
decipher. Zeno murmurs maxims beneath the hoarse shout of
Democritus; and though Democritus laugh loud and long, and the sneer
of Pyrrho be seen; yet, divine Plato, and Proclus, and Verulam are of my
counsel; and Zoroaster whispered me before I was born. I walk a world
that is mine; and enter many nations, as Mungo Park rested in African
cots; I am served like Baja-zet: Bacchus my butler, Virgil my minstrel,
Philip Sidney my page. My memory is a life beyond birth; my memory,
my library of the Vatican, its alcoves all endless perspectives, eve-tinted
by cross-lights from Middle-Age oriels.

And as the great Mississippi musters his watery nations: Ohio, with all
his leagued streams; Missouri, bringing down in torrents the clans from
the highlands; Arkansas, his Tartar rivers from the plain; – so, with all
the past and present pouring in me, I roll down my billow from
afar.   (*W*, III, pp. 367–368)

Imagining the great writers of the past as his minions and lackeys, Melville
recognizes his own talent and ambition but comes close to literary blasphemy.
Audacious they may be, these words represent some of Melville's greatest writing. *Mardi* is great only in selected passages, however. Before he could write at
his level best, he had to learn discipline and control, which he did with *Redburn*
and *White-Jacket*. Once he completed *White-Jacket*, he was ready to undertake
his finest work.

Confronting *Moby-Dick*

Melville exerted more control over the production of *Moby-Dick* than any of
his previous books. Before submitting the work for publication he took the
somewhat unusual step of arranging to have it stereotyped himself, a responsibility the publisher usually assumed. Several possible reasons motivated him –
the promise of greater profits, the hope of expediting publication, the possibility of avoiding the straight jacket of a publisher's house style, the chance to

circumvent an overfastidious editor, the ability to control the physical appearance of the finished book. His modern editors surmise that expedience principally motivated Melville to have the stereotype plates for *Moby-Dick* made himself (*W*, VI, p. 661). Concerns over the content and appearance of his book may have motivated him more. When it came to *Moby-Dick*, Melville not only wrote its text, he also helped shape its look.

As so many of his previous works show, Melville placed much importance on a book's front matter, which gives readers the first impression of the book as a whole. The early pages of *Moby-Dick* are more challenging than the confrontational prefaces that introduce some of his earlier books. In lieu of a preface, he supplied two separate sections, "Etymology" and "Extracts." The strange physical appearance of these sections in the first American edition of *Moby-Dick* reinforces themes Melville would develop throughout his story. To save space, subsequent editors have ignored the original layout and, consequently, have obscured the meaning embedded within the first American edition.

In the absence of external evidence, deciding which typographical decisions Melville made and which were made by his typesetter Robert Craighead is a tricky business. The typography of the dedication page, for example, is similar to the dedication page of John Henry Sherburne's *Life and Character of John Paul Jones*, a work Craighead stereotyped and printed the same year as *Moby-Dick*. The physical appearance of the rest of the front matter is unusual enough to suggest Melville's hand in its design, however.

Oddly, "Etymology" begins on the verso of the half-title page, a page usually left blank. Enclosed in parentheses beneath the word "Etymology" occurs the following statement in small caps: "Supplied by a late consumptive usher to a grammar school." A brief paragraph describing the behavior of this usher (schoolmaster's assistant) rounds out the page. In other words, the page does not actually contain the etymology; it only introduces the person who has supplied it. The facing page, also titled "Etymology," contains three definitions quoted from other sources and the word "whale" listed in various languages and orthographies. Placing the etymologist on one page and the etymology on the facing page, Melville suggested that a man's work is a reflection of himself and that man must face up to whatever he does. Turn over the leaf and find two similar pages, both titled "Extracts."

The first "Extracts" page describes a sub-sub-librarian who has commonplaced many quotations about whales and whaling from numerous literary and historical sources. The initial mention of Sub-Sub appears in black letter, an old-fashioned typeface prefiguring Melville's personification of a black letter text later in the book. The quotations themselves do not begin until the next page. Not only do the two facing "Extracts" pages reinforce the parallel between a man and his work, together they provide a double for the two facing "Etymology" pages. And Sub-Sub is a double for the consumptive usher.

These opening leaves establish a double motif that runs through the novel. Despite the numerous doubles that occur throughout its text, *Moby-Dick* is not typically read as a doppelgänger tale – though filmmaker Joseph Losey adumbrated such an interpretation by placing a copy of *Moby-Dick* in the hands of Alain Delon, who plays the title character in *Monsieur Klein*, a doppelgänger tale set during the Holocaust. Unlike *Monsieur Klein*, *Moby-Dick* does not contain a single set of doubles. Rather, multiple sets of doubles appear only to split and give rise to even more doubles.

Ishmael has a double-making personality. He appreciates life as something to be studied, contemplated, and solved. His compulsion to solve mysteries prompts him to identify closely with whatever or whomever he encounters. What he sees becomes a reflection of his mind. He thoroughly enjoys the challenge of examining the surface of things to try and discern what lies beneath. Ishmael is flaneur, phrenologist, and physiognomist. Throughout *Moby-Dick*, he never stops observing or trying to understand what things mean.

Beginning *Moby-Dick* with such unusual front matter, Melville presented his reader with a puzzle. The reader, too, becomes a double for Ishmael. Both are engaged in the process of solving a mystery. Like Ishmael, the reader tries to get an idea of the whole by interpreting its surface. As in Melville's earlier books, the front matter of *Moby-Dick* possesses the quality of a face, making the reader a physiognomist. Printed at the beginning of *Moby-Dick*, the letters, words, and sentences that form "Etymology" and "Extracts" are the wrinkles on the face of *Moby-Dick*, the first signs that allow the reader to begin understanding what this book means.

The front matter in *Moby-Dick* presents a challenge to the reader tantamount to a rite of initiation, a challenge some have been unwilling to take. Richard Bentley, realizing that readers might be put off by the front matter, moved both "Etymology" and "Extracts" to the back of the first English edition of the work, thus defeating their purpose. Though the use of an opening series of extracts was not unprecedented in English literature – think of Robert Southey's *The Doctor* – Bentley correctly surmised how people would react. An Englishman who read the first American edition took issue with Melville's front matter. Speaking of "Extracts," he commented, "It is having oil, mustard, vinegar, and pepper served up as a dish, in place of being scientifically administered sauce-wise" (*CR*, p. 382).

One contemporary reader who accepted Melville's challenge and enjoyed the book found a different food comparison appropriate: "There are people who delight in mulligatawny. They love curry at its warmest point. Ginger cannot be too hot in the mouth for them. Such people, we should think, constitute the admirers of Herman Melville" (*CR*, p. 365). *Moby-Dick* demands readers who are unafraid to confront the strange and unusual, those willing to use their minds, if not their palates, to face the mysteries of existence as reflected through an epic whaling quest.

Another set of doubles becomes apparent in the early chapters of *Moby-Dick*. The young Ishmael who travels aboard the *Pequod* is a double for the sadder and wiser Ishmael who narrates the story. Retelling the story of forecastle Ishmael, narrator Ishmael elevates his personal story of life aboard the *Pequod* into a compelling drama of extraordinary proportions. Walter Bezanson, who initiated the two-Ishmaels theory, hesitated to associate *Moby-Dick* with other doppelgänger tales, but the parallel between the older and younger selves becomes explicit quite early in the book, as the second chapter gives way to the third. In Chapter 2, "The Carpet-Bag," Ishmael describes making his way from New York to New Bedford, Massachusetts, where he arrives at the door of the Spouter Inn on a cold December evening. The chapter ends with him saying, "Let us scrape the ice from our frosted feet, and see what sort of a place this 'Spouter' may be" (*W*, VI, p. 11). Telling his story, the older Ishmael slips into the mindset of his younger self. The two seem one and the same.

In the following chapter, "The Spouter-Inn," the older Ishmael distances himself from the younger one by using the second person: "Entering that gable-ended Spouter-Inn, you found yourself in a wide, low, straggling entry with old-fashioned wainscots, reminding one of the bulwarks of some condemned old craft" (*W*, VI, p. 12). Ishmael's use of the second person also introduces some ambiguity. Besides addressing his younger self, he also seems to address the reader, who can thus vicariously enter the inn as Ishmael. The ambiguity reinforces the parallel between Ishmael and the reader.

Inside the Spouter Inn, Ishmael exemplifies his characteristic puzzle-solving behavior. In the entryway he sees a mysterious painting that demands careful scrutiny or, as he says, "much and earnest contemplation, and oft repeated ponderings" (*W*, VI, p. 12). He even opens a small window to shed some light on the painting. Few episodes better illustrate Ishmael's characteristic thought process. Once an object captures his attention, he cannot tear himself away until he ponders every possible meaning. Thinking for him is a slow, careful, deliberately-paced activity. He takes nothing for granted. Instead, he considers many possibilities and attempts to reconcile them as he gradually forms his interpretation.

Peter Coffin, the inn's proprietor, has no spare rooms, so he asks Ishmael if he would be willing to share a bed with a harpooneer. This circumstance creates further opportunities for reflection on Ishmael's part – and much opportunity for humor. The odd sleeping arrangement was a stock situation of humorous magazine fiction in Melville's day, and he exploits it to the fullest. Peter Coffin's playful banter and Ishmael's uncertainty about sharing a room with a stranger named Queequeg coalesce to form the first of many hilarious episodes in *Moby-Dick*.

Ishmael lingers in the public room late into the evening awaiting the harpooneer's return. With no sign of him, Peter Coffin lets him into Queequeg's room. Inside, Ishmael finds a poncho – a clue that may help solve the mystery of Queequeg. Explaining how he reacted to the poncho, Ishmael recalls, "I took it up, and held it close to the light, and felt it, and smelt it, and tried every way possible to arrive at some satisfactory conclusion concerning it." He even pulls the poncho over his head to see how it fits. Adorned in Queequeg's poncho, Ishmael looks at himself in the mirror: "I never saw such a sight in my life. I tore myself out of it in such a hurry that I gave myself a kink in the neck" (*W*, VI, p. 20).

This episode contributes to the humor, but it also has serious implications for one of the book's central themes and one of Melville's central concerns, the relationship between exterior appearance and what lies within. Ishmael is frightened at the sight of himself wearing the poncho because he realizes how fluid identity can be. He sees how easily he could slip into a state of savagery. Ishmael's mirror image is both himself and someone else, someone scary and frightening.

Putting Ishmael in Queequeg's poncho, Melville also laid the groundwork for turning Queequeg into another doppelgänger for Ishmael. As Queequeg enters their room toward the end of "The Spouter-Inn," the bizarre appearance of his tattoo-covered body sends Ishmael into hysterics. By the time the chapter ends, however, Ishmael has reconciled himself to spending the night in the same bed with him. He concludes, "What's all this fuss I have been making about, thought I to myself – the man's a human being just as I am: he has just as much reason to fear me, as I have to be afraid of him. Better sleep with a sober cannibal than a drunken Christian" (*W*, VI, p. 24).

The disparity between Queequeg's frightening appearance and his fundamental good nature leads Ishmael to discount facial tattoos as he attempts to physiognomize and phrenologize Queequeg. In Chapter 10, "A Bosom Friend," Ishmael explains, "You cannot hide the soul. Through all his unearthly tattooings, I thought I saw the traces of a simple honest heart; and in his large, deep eyes, fiery black and bold, there seemed tokens of a spirit that would dare a thousand devils" (*W*, VI, pp. 49–50). At this point, Ishmael still believes that personality can be discerned from outward appearance, but Queequeg's tattoos initially form a barrier to interpretation. Only by overlooking these man-made features can Ishmael see Queequeg's natural, God-given attributes and thus form an opinion of him.

Phrenologizing Queequeg, Ishmael compares his head to George Washington's: "It had the same long regularly graded retreating slope from above the brows, which were likewise very projecting, like two long promontories thickly wooded on top. Queequeg was George Washington cannibalistically developed" (*W*, VI, p. 50). Throughout *Moby-Dick*, and, indeed, throughout his work as a whole, Melville emphasized the essential dignity and equality of all men regardless of background, class, culture, nationality, or race. The comparison between a cannibal and one of America's founding fathers may shock some readers, but it serves to underscore the fundamental humanity they share.

Ishmael and Queequeg sail together from New Bedford to Nantucket. This brief trip provides an indication of how Queequeg will act on their longer voyage. When one passenger accidentally goes overboard, Queequeg, who had formerly teased the man, now risks his own life to rescue him. After the incident, Ishmael looks at Queequeg and imagines what he must be saying to himself: "It's a mutual, joint-stock world, in all meridians. We cannibals must help these Christians" (*W*, VI, p. 62). Once they get settled in Nantucket, Queequeg asks Ishmael to find a ship for both of them. Ishmael chooses the *Pequod* and goes aboard to meet the owners, Captain Peleg and Bildad – another hilarious encounter.

Ishmael returns to the *Pequod* with Queequeg in Chapter 18, "His mark." Unable to sign his name, Queequeg copies onto the paper "an exact counterpart of a queer round figure which was tattooed upon his arm" (*W*, VI, p. 89). The verbal description is vivid enough for readers to imagine Queequeg's mark, but Melville found it necessary to include a typographical symbol to represent it. What appears on the printed page, however, is not a queer round figure at all, but a cross patee. Often featured in heraldry and associated with chivalric knights, Queequeg's cross patee further blurs the boundaries between cannibal and Christian. The symbol casts Queequeg in the role of crusader. He is not a champion of Christianity, however; he symbolically defends the dignity of all men. Furthermore, the disparity between Melville's description of Queequeg's tattoo and the typographical symbol forces readers to continue questioning the validity of what they are reading. Print provides only a rough approximation of what an author means.

Melville returns to the theme of body decoration, once he introduces Captain Ahab. The typically short chapters between the appearance of the *Pequod* and Ahab's appearance help set the scene, enhance the mood, and introduce the other principal characters. Once Ishmael and Queequeg sign aboard the *Pequod*, they encounter Elijah, a prophet who foretells their doom. Elijah's presence creates a mood of dark foreboding. Subsequent travel writers would make use of this same motif. Frederick Dellenbaugh, for example, includes a crazy prophet in *Canyon Voyage*. Once at sea, Ishmael introduces the ship's three mates – Starbuck, Stubb, and Flask – the other harpooneers – Daggoo and Tashtego – and, finally, Ahab, the monomaniacal captain who is bent on avenging Moby Dick for the loss of his leg.

Like Queequeg's, Ahab's body contains external markings. Unlike Queequeg's tattoos, Ahab's body decorations are erasable. His prosthetic leg has a special blank space where he can take notes and do some ciphering. In Chapter 34, "The Cabin Table," Ishmael describes Ahab's behavior upon taking a measurement. He reckons the latitude "on the smooth, medallion-shaped tablet, reserved for that daily purpose on the upper part of his ivory leg" (*W*, VI, p. 149). The chapter title is a double entendre. Ostensibly about the captain's dinner table – an "ivory-inlaid table" – it also refers to Ahab's ivory tablet. Melville's inspiration for this idea came from pocket notebooks made from ivory. These ivory table books, as they were called, had the advantage of portability and erasability. They could be carried in the pocket and easily inscribed, erased, and reinscribed. Thomas Jefferson kept his accounts on an ivory table book, and Benjamin Franklin used one to maintain his careful plan for self-examination.

Such table books had a longstanding tradition as literary motifs, too. In *Hamlet*, to choose a literary work that exerted an important influence on *Moby-Dick*, Hamlet makes figurative and literal use of table books within the course of a single speech. The knowledge that Claudius has murdered his own brother destroys the concept of the world Hamlet has formed, and he resolves to erase his mind like a table book: "Yea, from the table of my memory / I'll wipe away all trivial fond records, / All saws of books, all forms, all pressures past / That youth and observations copied there." Hamlet's recognition of Claudius's duplicity prompts him to make an addition to his table book: "O villain, villain, smiling damned villain! My tables – meet it is I set it down / That one may smile, and smile, and be a villain!"

Unlike Hamlet, Ahab cannot erase the table of his memory. The injury he suffered by Moby Dick is forever inscribed in his mind. Like *Hamlet*, *Moby-Dick* confirms that one may smile and be a villain. Appearances *are* deceiving. Ahab proves much more difficult for Ishmael to read than Queequeg. With an ivory table book as part of his body, Ahab can mark himself with exterior markings visible for all to read. Inscribing his leg with measurements of latitude and longitude, Ahab lets others know exactly where he stands. Once he erases his ivory tablet, however, he displays a blank and unreadable space. Ahab's ivory tablet suggests the impossibility of discerning personality on the basis of external features.

Chapter 36, "The Quarter-Deck," marks the culmination of the first of *Moby-Dick*'s three movements. (The musical analogy is appropriate: Not only is a crucial chapter entitled "A Symphony," but *Moby-Dick* has inspired several important musical compositions including one of the great works of modern Italian music, Giorgio Federico Ghedini's *Concerto dell'albatro*, which quotes from Chapter 42, "The Whiteness of the Whale," at a climactic moment.) The second movement, nearly twice as long as the first, recreates life aboard a whaling ship as the *Pequod* takes a number of other whales in its quest for the legendary white whale, Moby Dick. In "The Quarter-Deck," Ahab announces his quest to the crew, and nails a doubloon to the mast as a reward for the first crew member who spies the white whale. This gold coin is not mentioned again until Chapter 99, "The Doubloon," which initiates the third movement of *Moby-Dick*.

Like Ishmael, Captain Ahab also understands that the visible world holds deeper meanings, but his process of discerning what lies beneath the surface differs significantly. Whereas Ishmael is cerebral and contemplative, Ahab is visceral and violent. When he announces to the crew his intention to avenge the injury he has suffered by Moby Dick in "The Quarter-Deck," his first mate, is flabbergasted. Moby Dick was simply a dumb animal acting on pure instinct when it bit off Ahab's leg, Starbuck insists. Ahab refuses to accept the idea that Moby Dick's behavior was motivated solely by instinct. The white whale's actions meant something more. "All visible objects, man, are but as pasteboard masks," Ahab tells him. "But in each event – in the living act, the undoubted deed – there, some unknown but still reasoning thing puts forth the mouldings of its features from behind the unreasoning mask. If man will strike, strike through the mask! How can the prisoner reach outside except by thrusting through the wall? To me, the white whale is that wall, shoved near to me" (*W*, VI, p. 164). Ahab's powerful words have resonated with some of Melville's most sensitive readers. Robert Louis Stevenson, for one, alluded to this passage in *The Master of Ballantrae*. Conveying his dislike of the title character, Stevenson's narrator recalls, "I had moments when I thought of him as of a man of pasteboard – as though, if one should strike smartly through the buckram of his countenance, there would be found a mere vacuity within."

Ahab's understanding of Moby Dick, contrasted with Ishmael's interpretation of the painting at the Spouter Inn, reveals how the two characters differ. Ishmael is calm and patient. He stares at the painting as long as necessary to interpret what it means. He has no qualms about making whatever physical adjustments are needed to facilitate his interpretive process. Though the paint-ing is located in a narrow entryway, the restrictions of the physical space do not constrain Ishmael's thoughts. His mind expands as his interpretation develops. Ahab, in contrast, is all impatience. Though his pursuit of Moby Dick occurs in the vast expanse of the ocean, he nevertheless feels claustrophobic. The white whale's existence seems like a wall closing in on him. For Ahab, understanding the deeper meanings does not involve contemplating its external appearance. Instead, it requires direct, and violent, action: breaking through the exterior to uncover what lies beneath.

Two parallel chapters, "Moby Dick" and "The Whiteness of the Whale," fur-ther contrast Ishmael and Ahab. The earlier chapter tells what the whale means to Ahab. Moby Dick represents "all his intellectual and spiritual exasperations" (*W*, VI, p. 184). As Orson Welles observed in his stage adaptation, *Moby Dick Rehearsed*, the whale in *Moby-Dick* resembles the storm in *King Lear*: "It's real, but it's more than real; – it's an idea of the mind." To Ahab, Moby Dick is "the monomaniac incarnation of all those malicious agencies which some deep men feel eating in them, till they are left living on with half a heart and half a lung." Continuing to develop this theme, Ishmael explains:

> All that most maddens and torments; all that stirs up the lees of things; all truth with malice in it; all that cracks the sinews and cakes the brain; all the subtle demonisms of life and thought; all evil, to crazy Ahab, were visibly personified, and made practically assailable in Moby Dick. He piled upon the whale's white hump the sum of all the general rage and hate felt by his whole race from Adam down; and then, as if his chest had been a mortar, he burst his hot heart's shell upon it.   (*W*, VI, p. 184)

This passage adds another dimension to Ahab's interpretive process, which is not just a matter of striking through but piling on. Ahab understands Moby Dick by projecting his own rage onto it. Moby Dick gradually becomes a reflection of Ahab.

In contrast to what the whale means to Ahab, Ishmael explains what it means to him in "The Whiteness of the Whale." This, Eisenstein's favorite chapter, has also been a favorite of many readers since *Moby-Dick* first appeared. Henry Chorley, one of the book's earliest reviewers, found the chapter "full of ghostly suggestions for which a Maturin or a Monk Lewis would have been thankful." Another contemporary reader said that the chapter "should be read at midnight, alone, with nothing heard but the sounds of the wind moaning without, and the embers falling into the grate within" (*CR*, pp. 357, 371).

"The Whiteness of the Whale" consists of a series of associations and reflec-tions conjured up in Ishmael's mind as he thinks about what white symbolizes.

Some of Ishmael's associations come from ancient myth and medieval European legend; others derive from American culture. Melville's specific examples reinforce his efforts to forge a unique American mythology. He mentions the white belt of wampum, which represents "the deepest pledge of honor"; the midwinter sacrifice of the sacred white dog among the Iroquois; the white steed of the Prairies, a legendary creature Melville knew from Josiah Gregg's *Commerce of the Prairies*; and the dread a backwoodsman feels as he understands the "comparative indifference" reflected by "an unbounded prairie sheeted with driven snow, no shadow of tree or twig to break the fixed trance of whiteness" (*W*, VI, pp. 188–195). To Ishmael, the white whale is not any of these things but all of them. Unlike Ahab, he feels no compulsion to derive a single answer to explain the white whale. His multifaceted interpretation reflects his personality. He remains open-minded, curious to solve the mysteries he confronts but uncompelled to devise a single solution.

Even after cataloguing the numerous things and ideas associated with the color white, Ishmael wonders if its essential emptiness – the absence of color – is what makes it most frightening. Its paradoxical nature contributes to its frightening power, too: white is not only the absence of color, it is also the combination of all colors of light. Up to this point in the book, Ishmael has established a pattern of interpreting objects by their appearance. Generally speaking, Ishmael copes by observing, interpreting what he observes, and then reconciling himself to whatever he encounters. Devoid of identifying marks, whiteness prevents a crucial part of Ishmael's interpretive process: reading the surface of things to see what they mean. No wonder he finds whiteness so frightening.

The "Moby Dick" chapter and "The Whiteness of the Whale" present completely different ideas about what the whale means, but they nonetheless serve to parallel Ishmael and Ahab, who is partly a reflection of Ishmael, too. Purportedly explaining what the whale meant to Ahab, the "Moby Dick" chapter really explains what Ishmael thinks the whale meant to Ahab. Though a first-person narrator, Ishmael often seems more like a third-person omniscient narrator. In Chapter 46, "Surmises," he goes so far as to claim the right to enter Ahab's thought processes. From this chapter through the last, Ishmael frequently explains what Ahab said and felt, even when he was not around to hear what Ahab was saying or to discern what he was feeling.

Just as it is important to distinguish the young Ishmael who sails aboard the *Pequod* from the old Ishmael who narrates the story of his younger self, it is also important to distinguish quarterdeck Ahab from tragic hero Ahab. The real and the ideal do not coincide. Ishmael admits that the Ahab he depicts is an embellished version of the real one. He deliberately contrasts the original

Ahab with the protagonist of the book he is writing: "But Ahab, my Captain, still moves before me in all his Nantucket grimness and shagginess; and in this episode touching Emperors and Kings, I must not conceal that I have only to do with a poor old whale-hunter like him; and, therefore, all outward majestical trappings and housings are denied me. Oh, Ahab! what shall be grand in thee, it must needs be plucked at from the skies, and dived for in the deep, and featured in the unbodied air!" (*W*, VI, p. 148). Ahab's tragic grandeur comes only through Ishmael's retelling of the tale.

Though the second movement of *Moby-Dick* contains such great chapters as "The Whiteness of the Whale," this part of the book has given some readers the fits. George Santayana, for one, confessed to getting stuck in the middle of *Moby-Dick*. For the true Melville aficionado, however, the second movement is beautifully paced. During the long middle portion of *Moby-Dick*, Archibald MacMechan observed, the reader "is infected with the leisurely, trade-wind, whaling atmosphere, and has no desire to proceed faster than at the *Pequod's* own cruising rate." Hart Crane disliked the second movement upon first reading *Moby-Dick*, but after reading it three or four times, he came to realize the aesthetic value of Melville's detail: "No work as tremendous and tragic as *Moby-Dick* can be expected to build up its ultimate tension and impact without manipulating our time sense to a great extent" (*Doubloon*, pp. 173, 116, 177).

The second movement makes reference to multiple whales taken by the *Pequod*, but it is structured according to a single chase and depicts the entire process of whaling, from lowering the boats to rendering the whale blubber. Typically, Ishmael describes one or another aspect of the whaling process, which provides an opportunity for wide-ranging reflections. The more he thinks about a subject, the more he is able to say and the farther he is able to soar. In Chapter 67, "Cutting In," for example, Ishmael describes the process of removing a whale's flesh, which spirals off the body in a long strip known as the blanket. This long piece of blubber forms the subject for the following chapter, "The Blanket," which explores the nature of a whale's skin.

"The Blanket" reiterates the theme of appearance versus reality and attempts to interpret the surface of a whale in order to understand the creature within. Initially, Ishmael ponders the nature of a whale's skin. He first mentions "an infinitely thin, transparent substance, somewhat resembling the thinnest shreds of isinglass" but concludes that this stuff is not the whale's skin. Still, it does give him an opportunity for reflection. He has saved some dried bits of it, which he now uses for bookmarks in his whaling books. Laid atop the printed page, these transparent bookmarks seem to magnify the text. Ishmael concludes that "it is pleasant to read about whales through their own spectacles, as you may say" (*W*, VI, pp. 305–306). Ishmael's bookmarks not only parallel the whale hunt with intellectual pursuit, they also reinforce the parallel between reading the printed page and interpreting the surface of an object. Furthermore, Ishmael's words extend the doppelgänger motif by drawing a general parallel between man and whale, which broadens the specific parallel between Ahab and Moby Dick.

Ishmael asserts that the blubber itself is the whale's skin. Having established the certainty of this assertion to his satisfaction, he next considers the strange markings on the whale's skin. The visible surface of the sperm whale, he explains, is "obliquely crossed and re-crossed with numberless straight marks in thick array, something like those in the finest Italian line engravings." The hieroglyphical markings that appear atop these engravings Ishmael compares to "the old Indian characters chiseled on the famous hieroglyphic palisades on the banks of the Upper Mississippi. Like those mystic rocks, too, the mystic-marked whale remains undecipherable" (*W*, VI, p. 306). Melville's comparison draws an analogy between the pursuit of the whale and the frontiersman's exploration of the American West. Each of Ishmael's reflections expands the figurative possibilities of the whale hunt. In Melville's hands, the pursuit of Moby Dick becomes an analogy for any pursuit man undertakes, for every pursuit man undertakes.

Unable to decipher the whale's exterior markings, Ishmael explores the blanket from a different angle. He compares it to an Indian poncho. This comparison recalls the time Ishmael tried on Queequeg's poncho and reinforces the parallel between man and whale. By the chapter's end, Ishmael apostrophizes man, urging him to pattern himself on the whale: "Oh, man! admire and model thyself after the whale! Do thou, too, remain warm among ice. Do thou, too, live in this world without being of it. Be cool at the equator; keep thy blood fluid at the Pole. Like the great dome of St. Peter's, and like the great whale, retain, O man! in all seasons a temperature of thine own" (*W*, VI, p. 307).

In Chapter 79, "The Prairie," – the chapter title refers to the vast expanse of the whale's forehead – Ishmael attempts to physiognomize the whale, but he concludes that it is virtually impossible: "If then, Sir William Jones, who read in thirty languages, could not read the simplest peasant's face in its profounder and more subtle meanings, how may unlettered Ishmael hope to read the awful Chaldee of the Sperm Whale's brow? I but put that brow before you. Read it if you can." While suggesting the impossibility of reading the whale's face, Ishmael nonetheless challenges the reader to try. In the next chapter, "The Nut," he resumes his own interpretive process by trying to phrenologize the whale.

Partway into "The Nut" he must admit that phrenology, too, is inadequate for the task at hand: "It is plain, then, that phrenologically the head of this Leviathan, in the creature's living intact state, is an entire delusion. As for his true brain, you can then see no indications of it, nor feel any. The whale, like all things that are mighty, wears a false brow to the common world" (*W*, VI, pp. 346–347, 349).

Ishmael has reached an understanding of the possibilities and limitations of physiognomy and phrenology. Looking past facial tattoos, he is able to understand Queequeg by the shape of his skull and the features of his face. The sperm whale, however, possesses a greatness that escapes interpretation. Similarly, great men also elude interpretation. The physical limits of the human skull mask the greatness of the mind it contains.

If great things and great men are ultimately impenetrable, then why does Ishmael persist in his interpretive efforts? He has an idea that everything means something. In "The Doubloon," he asserts, "And some certain significance lurks in all things, else all things are little worth, and the round world itself but an empty cipher, except to sell by the cartload, as they do hills about Boston, to fill up some morass in the Milky Way" (*W*, VI, p. 430). Ishmael sounds like he is trying to reassure himself. If there is no meaning beneath the surface of things, then the universe is indeed a bleak and empty place.

"The Doubloon" takes as its general theme the subjectivity of interpretation. Coming immediately after the last chapter about the process of whaling, this chapter serves to refocus the narrative, bringing all the principal characters together and reminding them of their quest. Each character approaches the doubloon and interprets the coin's face. Their interpretations vary wildly, but that is Melville's point. Anything we attempt to see is a combination of what it is and what we understand it to be. Essentially, "The Doubloon" celebrates interpretive subjectivity. If personal interpretation were reduced to a set of objective standards, the results would be horrific. Recall the opening sequence of *Monsieur Klein*. A Nazi physician precisely measures the features of a naked woman to compare them with pre-established standard measurements in order to determine if she is Semitic. Whether she conforms to the standards will determine whether she lives or dies.

"The Doubloon" universalizes what Ishmael has been doing throughout the book, namely, interpreting his experience subjectively. As Ishmael develops the story of Captain Ahab's pursuit of Moby Dick, the two almost become one. In the late chapters, Ishmael emphasizes the physical features Ahab and Moby Dick share. Both have deeply furrowed brows. In Chapter 113, "The Forge," Ahab asks Perth the blacksmith to smooth out his forehead, but Perth tells him that a wrinkled brow is the one thing he cannot smooth out. Ahab realizes why his forehead is unsmoothable. He tells Perth that his wrinkled brow "has worked down into the bone of my skull – *that* is all wrinkles!" Similarly, Ishmael emphasizes the furrowed brow of Moby Dick on multiple occasions, most forcefully in the final chapter, "The Chase – Third Day." Moby Dick's forehead appears menacing: "The wide tiers of welded tendons overspreading his broad white forehead, beneath the transparent skin, looked knitted together" (*W*, VI, pp. 488, 567). As Ahab confronts Moby Dick, two wrinkled brows face one another.

Joseph Losey's inclusion of *Moby-Dick* in *Monsieur Klein* functions as a gloss on Melville's story. When Alain Delon goes in search of his other self, he looks through his double's flat, where he finds a copy of *Moby-Dick*. When Captain Ahab goes in search of Moby Dick, he ends up confronting his other self. Additional analogues are possible. When Ishmael tells the story of Moby Dick, he confronts his younger self. And as we, Melville's readers, read *Moby-Dick*, we end up confronting ourselves.

The interpretation of *Moby-Dick* as doppelgänger tale need not be pushed further. Like any critical interpretation of the book, it enlightens only one aspect of a complex work that no single interpretation can fully encompass. "To produce a mighty book, you must choose a mighty theme" (*W*, VI, p. 456). This, one of Ishmael's finest maxims, reflects Melville's intent with *Moby-Dick*, a mighty book that takes hold of the imagination and refuses to let go. What Oakey Hall said about *Pierre* applies equally to *Moby-Dick*. When you finish reading it, "the book gradually falls from the hand, while in reverie your own imagination upon the author's steed – late rider being dismounted – travels farther and farther on in the regions of speculation" (*CR*, p. 433).

The images and ideas Melville expressed in *Moby-Dick* linger in the minds of his readers long after they have finished the book. To list a few: the sermon inspired by the Book of Jonah that Father Mapple preaches; the contrasting folk sermon that Fleece, the *Pequod*'s cook, delivers to the voracious sharks that feed upon whale flesh; Ishmael's humorous attempt to break down the door of their room when Queequeg does not respond – a situation that would become a commonplace of American humor; the spirited revelry of "Midnight, forecastle"; the darkly foreboding tale of Radney and Steelkilt in "The Town-Ho's story"; the tender image of new-born whales in "The grand armada"; the intimate camaraderie with his fellow man Ishmael experiences in "A squeeze of the hand"; the sharp contrast between fire imagery and the surrounding darkness in "The try works"; the sight of St Elmo's fire descending from the *Pequod*'s yardarms, a natural phenomenon Ahab manipulates as his own; the gruesome image of the dead body of Fedallah roped to Moby

Dick, a suicide harpooner who has given his life in pursuit of a hopeless cause; the final image of Ahab in all his grandeur and glory, a picture Angela Carter found as pitiably fearful as Eisenstein's *Ivan the Terrible*; and the ear-piercing shrieks of the birds that circle overhead as the *Pequod* swirls into the sea.

Moby-Dick is chockful of enough memorable images and ideas to give every-one a favorite passage. Here's mine: "And there is a Catskill eagle in some souls that can alike dive down into the blackest gorges, and soar out of them again and become invisible in the sunny spaces. And even if he for ever flies within the gorge, that gorge is in the mountains; so that even in his lowest swoop the mountain eagle is still higher than other birds upon the plain, even though they soar" (*W*, VI, p. 425). It is humbling to try and say anything more after such majestic words. One further sentence must suffice: *Moby-Dick* is the greatest book in the history of the English language.

Pierre: the making of a tragic hero

What did Melville write after *Moby-Dick*? One might as well ask what Shake-speare wrote after *King Lear* or what Picasso painted after *Guernica*. What does any great artist do after creating a masterwork? Of questions like these, there is one that is easy to answer: What did Beethoven compose after his Fifth Symphony? Why, the Sixth Symphony, of course. Designated as part of a numerical series, each Beethoven symphony, a work of art in itself, also forms part of a greater oeuvre. The cinema provides a further example. When a friend complained that his most recent film was not his best, Martin Scorsese quipped, "Do we always have to make our best film each time or are we building an oeu-vre that will last?"[18] Perhaps all great artists reach a point in their careers when they start thinking less about individual works and more about their oeuvre. Melville reached this point before he completed *Moby-Dick*, his sixth book, and began his seventh, *Pierre; or, The Ambiguities*.

Moby-Dick let Melville realize the greatness of his literary powers and made him anxious to exercise them. Writing from Arrowhead during its composition, he made a fanciful request of Evert Duyckinck: "Can you send me about fifty fast-writing youths, with an easy style and not averse to polishing their labors? If you can, I wish you would, because since I have been here I have planned about that number of future works and cant find enough time to think about them separately." This sentence captures the creative enthusiasm Melville was experiencing. By the time the American edition of *Moby-Dick* appeared, he was ready to put the book behind him and start his next project. He wrote to

Hawthorne, "As long as we have anything more to do, we have done nothing. So, now, let us add Moby Dick to our blessing, and step from that. Leviathan is not the biggest fish; – I have heard of Krakens" (*W*, XIV, pp. 174, 213). Well on his way to completing *Pierre*, Melville foresaw this new book as similar to yet greater than *Moby-Dick*, much like the kraken, a mythological sea beast, was supposed to be greater than the greatest whale.

Linking *Moby-Dick* and *Pierre* together as two works that formed a significant part of his oeuvre, Melville realized that the later book could explore aspects of the tragic hero left unexplored in the earlier one. John Freeman called *Pierre* the spiritual counterpart to *Moby-Dick*.[19] To borrow a term from the cinema, *Pierre* can be seen as a kind of prequel to *Moby-Dick*. Before *Moby-Dick* begins, Captain Ahab has already lost his leg to a legendary white whale and set his mind on vengeance. In other words, he has already undergone the physical and mental tortures that have made him who he is. Recognizing that *Moby-Dick* had left unsaid the process a character undergoes on the way to becoming a tragic hero, Melville understood that he had the makings of a new and complementary book.

Pierre Glendinning's tragic fate is largely determined by his family and his community. Nineteen years old as the story begins, he makes his home in Saddle Meadows, a small community located in rural New England, where he lives in a large manor house with his widowed mother. Her husband, who passed away when Pierre was a boy, occupies a lofty place in the memory of his widow and the eyes of their son. To his surviving family, Mr Glendinning survives as the image of the perfect husband and father. His widow honors him whenever she can. Throughout Pierre's adolescence and teenage years, his father has remained a figure for him to idolize and emulate. For example, when Pierre begins to rant and rave one day his mother scolds him and suggests that he try to be more like his father. "Never rave, Pierre; and never rant," she tells him. "Your father never did either; nor is it written of Socrates; and both were very wise men" (*W*, VII, p. 19). Likening her husband's wisdom to the wisdom of Socrates, Mrs Glendinning shows how deeply she reveres him, how closely she expects Pierre to follow in his footsteps, and how utterly impossible it will be for Pierre to emulate his father.

A statue of Pierre's father erected on their property at Saddle Meadows takes on the quality of a religious shrine. The narrator's description of this statue reveals the depth of Pierre's filial piety: "In this shrine, in this niche of this pillar, stood the perfect marble form of his departed father; without blemish, unclouded, snow-white, and serene; Pierre's fond personification of perfect human goodness and virtue" (*W*, VII, p. 68). Whereas his mother compares her husband to Socrates, Pierre makes him seem more like

Jesus. Either way, Mr Glendinning symbolizes both goodness and greatness. Pierre idealizes him to such an extent that when dark secrets cast shadows on his father's past, Pierre can scarcely reconcile them with the image he has formed.

Pierre's understanding of his father is unrealistic; his relationship with his mother is unnatural. The two are so close it's creepy. Instead of calling her mother, Pierre calls her sister. In turn, she addresses him as brother. They behave toward one another less like mother and son or sister and brother and more like boyfriend and girlfriend. Pierre especially enjoys helping his mother get dressed. One morning, he wraps a ribbon around her neck and fastens it with a kiss. *Pola X*, Léos Carax's film adaptation, captures the mood of Melville's original. (The film's title is formed from the acronym to the French title, *Pierre; ou les ambiguities.*) In one scene, Pierre nonchalantly enters the bathroom while his mother, played by Catherine Deneuve, is bathing.

Since her husband's death, Mrs Glendinning has had a number of suitors both young and old. Pierre reacts to them like a jealous lover. The narrator explains, "Pierre had more than once, with a playful malice, openly sworn, that the man – gray-beard, or beardless – who should dare to propose marriage to his mother, that man would by some peremptory unrevealed agency immediately disappear from the earth" (*W*, VII, p. 5). The unconventional relationship Pierre has with his mother shapes his attitude toward other relationships, frees him from social convention, and paves the way for the bizarre decision he makes in the face of an experience unprecedented in his life.

Though he enjoys calling his mother his sister, Pierre regrets not having a real sister as the story begins. According to his image of the ideal family, a brother must have a sister to make the family complete. Pierre is saddened because "so delicious a feeling as fraternal love" has been denied him. Voicing what Pierre feels, the narrator observes, "He who is sisterless, is as a bachelor before his time. For much that goes to make up the deliciousness of a wife, already lies in the sister" (*W*, VII, p. 7). Pierre's longing makes it much easier for him to accept the mysterious young woman who enters his life claiming to be his sister – regardless of the consequences.

The community contributes to Pierre's tragic heroism by creating and enforcing a narrow set of values which the people of Saddle Meadows must follow. With Saddle Meadows, Melville took the opportunity to do something he had yet to do in his literary career. In previous works, he had excelled in depicting the sailor's life aboard a variety of different ship-board communities from the merchant vessel in *Redburn* to the man-of-war in *White-jacket* and the whaling ship in *Moby-Dick*. With *Pierre*, he tried his hand at recreating life within a rural community. He had numerous literary precedents. The rural setting, complete with the young man of the manor house, the haughty mother, the beautiful village girl, and the bumbling vicar, were well-established conventions of the English novel. In American literature, the plantation novels of the antebellum South gave Melville additional examples to follow. Despite such models, Melville ran into difficulties as he tried to recreate a typical rural community in *Pierre*. In terms of moral stance, both the English novels and the Southern plantation novels were conservative: they sought to conserve the values the community represented. In *Pierre*, Melville shakes the community to its foundations, challenging and ultimately destroying the values it represents.

Typically, the tragic hero occupies a prominent place in the community. Codifying the general tenets of tragedy in his *Poetics*, Aristotle stressed that the tragic hero should be a man of high reputation or a famous member of an important family. Whereas *Moby-Dick* had challenged this traditional pattern by turning a whaleman into a tragic hero, Pierre Glendinning, as heir to the most prominent family in the community, conforms to literary tradition. But Pierre's tragic flaw prohibits him from functioning according to the narrowly defined standards of behavior the community represents. His idealism destines him to tragedy.

Other factors help turn Pierre into a tragic hero. The books he reads have helped make him who he is. Like Wellingborough Redburn, Pierre has devoted much time reading his way through his father's library. The narrator explains that Pierre has spent "long summer afternoons in the deep recesses of his father's fastidiously picked and decorous library." Here, the "Spenserian nymphs had early led him into many a maze of all-bewildering beauty" (*W*, VII, p. 6). His father's books give him a fanciful view of the world that has nothing to do with reality.

Nature has endowed Pierre with an innate heroic sense, too. Personifying nature as a woman, Melville wrote, "She whispered through her deep groves at eve, and gentle whispers of humanness, and sweet whispers of love, ran through Pierre's thought-veins, musical as water over pebbles. She lifted her spangled crest of a thickly-starred night, and forth at that glimpse of their divine Captain and Lord, ten thousand mailed thoughts of heroicness started up in Pierre's soul, and glared round for some insulted good cause to defend" (*W*, VII, p. 14). In short, Pierre was born to play the hero. Another natural facility – his imagination – contributes to his heroic tendency. In his mind, Pierre imagines the dangers that others face and sees himself as their hero and savior.

All of these various factors – the idealization of his dead father, the personal closeness with his mother, his longing for a sister to protect and defend, the severe restrictions the community imposes on moral conduct, the unrealistic view of the world his books present, and his natural tendency to play the hero – combine to give Pierre the potential to become a tragic hero. All he needs is a spark to set him off.

The spark is Isabel.

As the story begins, Pierre's future seems laid out for him: He will soon marry Lucy Tartan. The two will live in splendor and raise a large family. Pierre will grow old gracefully as he oversees Saddle Meadows. He will become what his father was and what his mother has always wanted him to be. But when Isabel, a mysterious young woman claiming to be his illegitimate sister comes to Saddle Meadows, Pierre's idyllic little world is shattered. Isabel's existence destroys Pierre's concept of his father, activates his innate sense of chivalry, and presents him with a dilemma. How can he bring Isabel into the family while preserving his mother's idealized view of her husband? Pierre reaches a momentous decision: he will pretend that he and Isabel have secretly married. He rationalizes this decision as the only possible way to resolve the dilemma he faces. While deciding what to do, however, Pierre never admits to himself his true motivation: he has fallen in love with his sister.

Once Pierre has made his decision, the House of Glendinning is bound to destruction as surely as the House of Usher in Poe's great story. Mrs Glendinning exiles Pierre from Saddle Meadows and perishes in his absence. Pierre and Isabel, along with Delly Ulver, a young local woman who has been seduced and abandoned, travel to New York City, where they find lodging in a squalid rookery. Lucy Tartan, whose broken heart brings her near death, makes a bizarre decision of her own. She comes to New York and moves in with Pierre and Isabel. Lucy's brother and Glen Stanly – Pierre's cousin – try to rescue her. The denouement is as swift and fatal as an Elizabethan revenger's tragedy.

Pierre is a lush book full of gorgeous, often extravagant prose. One particular episode in the story stands above the rest. Book XVI, "First night of their arrival in the city," describes the entry of Pierre, Isabel, and Delly to New York City. Not only does Book XVI present a pivotal episode in the story of Pierre Glendinning, it also forms a pivotal episode in the history of American literature and culture. Leaving the country behind in favor of the city, Pierre experiences what countless others would experience as the population shifted from rural to urban in the coming decades, during which time the move from country to city would become a prominent motif in many American novels.

At the start of Book XVI, the narrator of *Pierre* widens his distance from his hero. Unlike Pierre, the narrator is attuned to the rhythms of the city. Depicting the night Pierre enters New York City with Isabel and Delly, the narrator parallels the time of night with the behavior of the city's inhabitants:

"There was no moon and few stars. It was that preluding hour of the night when the shops are just closing, and the aspect of almost every wayfarer, as he passes through the unequal light reflected from the windows, speaks of one hurrying not abroad, but homeward" (*W*, VII, p. 229). Night modifies the rhythms of a city. Never having entered the city at night, Pierre cannot adjust to its nocturnal rhythms. His initial uneasiness manifests itself in the form of an abrasive critique of the city. Over the course of Book XVI, his personal discomfort shifts from dismay to rage.

Melville's use of chiaroscuro – the interplay of light and shadow – enhances the sense of foreboding. Describing the parallel rows of street lamps that lined the street before their coach, the narrator observes that these lamps "seemed not so much intended to dispel the general gloom, as to show some dim path leading through it, into some gloom still deeper beyond" (*W*, VII, p. 229). A fairly recent innovation, streetlamps, while designed to impose order on the night, destroy the uniformity of the darkness, create contrast, and effectively deepen the shadows.

While Book XVI begins with such striking visual imagery, it soon engages other senses, specifically the senses of touch and sound. When they reach the first stretch of cobblestones, the three feel "numerous hard, painful joltings." Never having been to the city, Isabel and Delly have never experienced cobblestones. When Isabel asks what the painful joltings mean, Pierre lets them know that they have entered the city. Delly comments that the cobbles do not feel "so soft as the green sward." Pierre's figurative response scarcely comforts Delly. He bitterly suggests that the cobbles are "the buried hearts of some dead citizens." Isabel wonders if city people are so hardhearted. Pierre maintains his tone: "Milk dropt from the milkman's can in December, freezes not more quickly on those stones, than does snow-white innocence, if in poverty, it chance to fall in these streets" (*W*, VII, p. 230). Realizing his bleak comments were upsetting Delly and Isabel, Pierre apologizes, but he cannot prevent a dark tone from creeping back as his discomfort and uneasiness increase.

After Pierre and Lucy got engaged, Glen Stanly had offered his town house as a place for them to stay in the city. Though Pierre had broken up with Lucy to feign marriage with Isabel, he foolishly assumed that Glen's offer still applied. Pierre had even written ahead with detailed instructions, telling Glen how to get the town house ready for them and even instructing him to purchase some specialized coffee. Bordering on the absurd, Pierre's detailed instructions show how out of touch he was with reality.

Once the coachman reaches the general vicinity of Glen's town house, he asks Pierre for the house number. Pierre does not know. He only knows the house by its appearance. It is a "small old-fashioned dwelling with stone lion-heads above the windows" (*W*, VII, p. 233). Like street lamps, house numbers were another modern urban innovation that had been unnecessary in a small community like Saddle Meadows. Showing his inability to negotiate the city streets by numbers, Pierre reveals his naiveté and unpreparedness. When the coachman jokes about his lack of knowledge, Pierre indignantly jumps from the coach, grabs the horses's reins, and abruptly brings the coach to a stop, refusing to travel any further with this indignant coachman.

Coincidentally, Pierre has stopped the coach right in front of the watch house for the local police. Like the street lamps and the cobbles, police were another aspect of the modern city that Saddle Meadows had lacked. There, as Delly's negative experience proved, the behavior of local residents was controlled by the community and the church. Though Pierre was rebelling against the all-too-stringent codes of behavior prevalent in Saddle Meadows, he had now reached a place where peer pressure and religious coercion in themselves could not control aberrant behavior. In the city, police are essential to keep order. Since the watch house is quiet, Pierre arranges with the police to leave Isabel and Delly here while he goes in search of transportation.

As Pierre enters the heart of the city, chiaroscuro gives way to technicolor. A streetwalker standing in "the flashing, sinister, evil cross-lights of a druggist's window" calls out to him as he passes. "Scarlet-cheeked, glaringly-arranged," she is "horribly lit by the green and yellow rays from the druggist's" (*W*, VII, p. 237). Pierre shudders at the sight of her. Speaking to himself, he sardonically calls her "the town's first welcome to youth!"

Pierre's encounter with this prostitute echoes Robin's experience in Nathaniel Hawthorne's "My kinsman, Major Molineux." Robin, too, accidentally meets a lady of the evening when he enters the city. There is a crucial difference between the two, however. While the two characters are about the same age, Pierre is at a different stage in life. Robin is like a bear cub that has yet to be licked into shape. As he enters the city, he remains a man in the making. Pierre is already fully formed as he enters the city. He may call himself a youth, but he has already made the decisions that will determine the rest of his life. Robin enters the city on his way up, Pierre on his way down. Instead of an earlier figure from American literature, perhaps a later one would make for a better comparison to Pierre. Think of George Hurstwood in *Sister Carrie*.

As he roams the city streets, Pierre happens to reach Glen Stanly's home. Glen has stationed a man at his door to prevent his entrance, yet Pierre barges in and approaches Glen, who pretends not to know him. Pierre is ready for a fight, but Glen has him physically removed from his home.

Back in the street, Pierre looks for a hack. Almost crazy with rage, he approaches some hackmen, who call him a rogue, something the quondam master of Saddle Meadows has never been called in his entire life. Pierre's personality is ebbing away in the city. Suddenly, he finds himself in the midst of several hacks and horses. The narrator explains, "This sudden tumultuous surrounding of him by whipstalks and lashes, seemed like the onset of the chastising fiends upon Orestes" (*W*, VII, p. 240). The Furies beset Orestes after he murdered his mother Clytemnestra and almost drove him mad. The comparison reinforces Pierre's behavior as a kind of matricide.

Pierre finally makes his way back to the watch house, which has filled up with prostitutes, pickpockets, and various other assorted kinds of lowlife. Melville's description is extraordinary:

> In indescribable disorder, frantic, diseased-looking men and women of all colors, and in all imaginable flaunting, immodest, grotesque, and shattered dresses, were leaping, yelling, and cursing around him. The torn Madras handkerchiefs of negresses, and the red gowns of yellow girls, hanging in tatters from their naked bosoms, mixed with the rent dresses of deep-rouged white women, and the split coats, checkered vests, and protruding shirts of pale, or whiskered, or haggard, or mustached fellows of all nations, some of whom seemed scared from their beds, and others seemingly arrested in the midst of some crazy and wanton dance. On all sides, were heard drunken male and female voices, in English, French, Spanish, and Portuguese, interlarded now and then, with the foulest of all human lingoes, that dialect of sin and death, known as the Cant language, or the Flash.   (*W*, VII, p. 240)

In Pierre's absence, Isabel and Delly have been engulfed in this sea of vile humanity. He heroically rescues them, and together they proceed to the relative safety of a nearby hotel.

Pierre's experiences this evening reveal what he has lost by his decision to run away with Isabel. Having renounced his family and his community, Pierre has renounced the very things that had determined his identity. The shift from uneasiness to rage to the brink of madness he undergoes in Book XVI offers an experience in miniature of what Pierre would experience in the remainder of his story. In Melville's hands, Pierre Glendinning became one of the great tragic heroes in literary history.

Private letters

Melville is among the finest letter writers in American literary history. This fact has so far gone unnoticed because Melville wrote fewer letters than any other major author in American literature. Though capable of writing great letters, seldom could he work himself up to it. Two conditions were essential to inspire his letter writing. He had to be in a mood of creative enthusiasm, and he needed a sympathetic correspondent, one who understood and appreciated what he was trying to say. His best letters date from that brief period of his life between the completion of *Mardi* and the start of *Pierre*. Writing to one favorite correspondent or another, he created a private little world for the two of them, a world in which he felt free to express his thoughts and fears about the literary life.

His first deeply sympathetic correspondent outside his family was Evert Duyckinck. One of Melville's best letters to Duyckinck comes after he finished *Mardi* but before its publication and disappointing reception. Responding to comments Duyckinck had made about Emerson, Melville explained, "I do not oscillate in Emerson's rainbow, but prefer rather to hang myself in mine own halter than swing in any other man's swing." The brief appreciation of Emerson which follows this sentence gives way to a generalization pertinent to other great minds: "I love all men who *dive*. Any fish can swim near the surface, but it takes a great whale to go down stairs five miles or more; and if he don't attain the bottom, why, all the lead in Galena can't fashion the plummet that will. I'm not talking of Mr Emerson now – but of the whole corps of thought-divers, that have been diving and coming up again with blood-shot eyes since the world began" (*W*, XIV, p. 121).

Diving was a favorite metaphor of Melville's. His comments in this letter anticipate his finest use of the metaphor: the Catskill eagle. In both instances, diving refers to plumbing the depths of the mind. In the letter, he enhanced the metaphor by giving it a more visceral quality, imbuing his figurative expression with graphic detail. Describing an aspect of a person who has literally dived too deep – blood-shot eyes – he suggested that thought divers must be willing to risk personal harm. As they engage the thinking process, they must put their egos and their psyches at risk to plumb their souls.

Like the most memorable passages in his books, Melville's best letters form chains of association that lead him far beyond where he started. Once Emerson gets him thinking about great minds, great minds bring him to William Shakespeare. Melville may not have oscillated in Emerson's rainbow, but in his own characteristic thought patterns, he did swing between the specific and the general as he cleared a way to think.

Instead of picturing Shakespeare in Renaissance England, Melville imagined him in modern-day New York promenading down Broadway and sipping punch at one of Duyckinck's famous literary soirees. But it was not for the opportunity to meet him that Melville wished to see Shakespeare in the nineteenth century. Were Shakespeare alive in modern times, he could express his thoughts more fully and more freely than he had in his own. No longer would he wear "the muzzle which all men wore on their souls in the Elizebethan day" (*W*, XIV, p. 122). Upon inscribing this statement, Melville wondered whether he had gone too far. The tone of his letter grows melancholy as its author realizes that even in modern America, no one, no matter how great, can speak the absolute truth. The shift from enthusiasm to melancholy is another characteristic pattern that recurs in Melville's letters.

Once he moved to Pittsfield in 1850, his new dwelling place offered material to amuse city-bound correspondents. In his earliest known letter to Duyckinck from Arrowhead, Melville revealed his new excitement for Shakespeare with a neologism derived from *As You Like It*. Living in the country let him spend entire days "*Jacquesizing* in the woods." In a letter to Duyckinck, dated the second week of December, he gloried in his surroundings: "I have a sort of sea-feeling here in the country, now that the ground is all covered with snow. I look out of my window in the morning when I rise as I would out of a port-hole of a ship in the Atlantic. My room seems a ship's cabin; and at nights when I wake up and hear the wind shrieking, I almost fancy there is too much sail on the house, and I had better go on the roof and rig in the chimney" (*W*, XIV, pp. 170, 173). This letter combines Melville's previous history and his present state in a humorous and charming way. Furthermore, his words form another characteristic pattern that recurs in both his private and public writings. After making a figurative comparison, he typically extended it to create a startling new idea.

Spending the winter in rural Massachusetts, Melville recognized the imaginative possibilities of snow, as another letter to Duyckinck confirms. Describing a visit to Hawthorne in nearby Lenox, he wrote, "I found him, of course, buried in snow; and the delightful scenery about him, all wrapped up and tucked away under a napkin, as it were" (*W*, XIV, p. 180). Melville's fanciful use of snow in his letters reflects his personal enjoyment of winter. His mother's correspondence confirms this attitude. One snowy, windy, frightfully cold Christmas Eve, Melville had the family sleigh brought around. Her explanation for his behavior seems almost matter-of-fact. Herman "loves to go out in such wild weather," she wrote.[20] Mrs Melville's boy might have made his reputation as a rover in the tropics, but he had a mind of winter.

The December 1850 letter to Duyckinck offers a day-in-the-life description, which constitutes one of the most idyllic passages in all of Melville's writings:

> Do you want to know how I pass my time? – I rise at eight – thereabouts – and go to my barn – say good-morning to the horse, and give him his breakfast. (It goes to my heart to give him a cold one, but it can't be

helped.) Then, pay a visit to my cow – cut up a pumpkin or two for her, and stand by to see her eat it – for it's a pleasant sight to see a cow move her jaws – she does it so mildly and with such a sanctity. – My own breakfast over, I go to my workroom and light my fire – then spread my M.S.S on the table – take one business squint at it, and fall to with a will. At $2^1/_2$ P.M. I hear a preconcerted knock at my door, which (by request) continues till I rise and go to the door, which serves to wean me effectively from my writing, however interested I may be. My friends the horse and cow now demand their dinner – and I go and give it them. My own dinner over, I rig my sleigh and with my mother or sisters start off for the village – and if it be a *Literary World* day, great is the satisfaction thereof. – My evenings I spend in a sort of mesmeric state in my room – not being able to read – only now and then skimming over some large-printed book.   (*W*, XIV, p. 174)

In this passage, Melville gives Duyckinck a peep into his writer's room, the inner sanctum where he closed the door behind him upon entering, where he lost himself in thought so deep that it took loud, insistent rapping to break his concentration. Though Melville could write very quickly, such speed came with a price. As he wrote he achieved a state of intense concentration. He could write without food. He could write without sleep. He could write to the point of mental and physical and spiritual exhaustion – and often did. In the words of Jean-Jacques Mayoux, Melville wrote like "a kind of barbaric Flaubert."[21] Letting his friend look into his writer's room, Melville was offering him a rare glimpse into a privileged place. Duyckinck, who had numerous literary correspondents, never fully realized how special Melville's letters were.

Melville typically gave his closest correspondents a little treat just for them. One of his most delightful letters is addressed to his sister Kate and playfully describes the beauties of all women named Kate. Besides the peep into his writer's room, Melville gave Duyckinck another treat by mentioning the *Literary World*, the weekly magazine he and his brother George edited. The letter's first reference to this magazine, which depicts its arrival in the mail as an event to celebrate, seems like a fanciful pose; the second reference is more revealing. Melville wrote, "In the country here, I begin to appreciate the *Literary World*. I read it as a sort of private letter from you to me" (*W*, XIV, p. 174). Intended as a compliment, the remark unwittingly reveals Melville's occasional reluctance to distinguish public and private writings.

Reading the *Literary World* as a private letter, something written by Duyckinck for his eyes only, Melville was fantasizing. In so doing, he was setting himself up for disappointment. To be sure, Duyckinck never forgot the public nature of his magazine. He erred in the opposite direction. Whereas Melville read the

Literary World as a private letter, Duyckinck tended to read private utterances as public. He frequently exploited his private literary correspondence to enhance his editorial work. His correspondents usually did not mind because his actions often worked to their mutual benefit. Melville resented Duyckinck's attempts to publicize his name, however. With neither the savvy nor the inclination to promote his own work, Melville took offense when Duyckinck took advantage of their friendship.

In one instance, Duyckinck asked him to contribute to an article to *Holden's Dollar Magazine*. To accompany the article, he requested that Melville submit a daguerreotype as the basis for a steel-engraved portrait. In a letter his biographer has called an "ambivalent, pugnacious, placating response," Melville refused to write the article and further refused to send Duyckinck a photograph.[22] He explained, "The fact is, almost everybody is having his 'mug' engraved nowadays; so that this test of distinction is getting to be reversed; and therefore, to see one's 'mug' in a magazine, is presumptive evidence that he's a nobody" (*W*, XIV, p. 180).

From Melville's perspective, Duyckinck had violated the trust underlying their personal correspondence, a private exchange between the two of them. He felt betrayed and exploited by Duyckinck's request for the portrait. The recent invention of photography further complicated the relationship between private and public. As Roland Barthes has explained, the beginnings of photography marked "the explosion of the private into the public, or rather into the creation of a new social value, which is the publicity of the private."[23] The daguerreotype initiated an era that continues today, a time when the visual image of a person plays a significant role in determining popular and professional reputation. Melville balked at the new demands the nascent cult of personality was creating. Though his integrity is admirable in retrospect, his reluctance to publicize himself hindered the sale of his novels and prevented many of the day's readers from becoming interested in his work.

Duyckinck's request for Melville's portrait did not ruin their relationship, but it anticipated the sharp break that would occur after *Moby-Dick* appeared. Duyckinck's negative review of the book hurt and angered Melville. In revenge, Melville dramatized Duyckinck's request for a daguerreotype in *Pierre*. He had turned the tables. Now he was exploiting their private correspondence in a published work.

After Duyckinck refused to help Melville find a publisher for *Pierre* in early 1852, Melville wrote a letter astonishing for its brevity and its formality. Instead of addressing him as "My dear Duyckinck," he addressed this letter to the "Editors of the Literary World." Its body consists of a single sentence: "You will please discontinue the two copies of your paper sent to J. M. Fly at Brattleboro' (or Greenbush), and to H Melville at Pittsfield" (*W*, XIV, p. 222). Almost a decade would pass before he and Duyckinck patched up their differences.

Before the break between the two, Melville had found a more sensitive and sympathetic correspondent: Nathaniel Hawthorne. Nearly every letter he wrote to Hawthorne is beautifully crafted. Take the one he wrote the third week of April 1851 for example. Written shortly after the publication of *The House of the Seven Gables*, the letter congratulates Hawthorne and offers an extended commentary on the book.

Melville's critical appreciation of Hawthorne's book is so delightful that one wishes he had written more literary criticism. But Melville could seldom bring himself to comment on the work of others publicly. As a personal favor to Duyckinck he had reviewed a handful of books for the *Literary World* – James Fenimore Cooper's *Red Rover*, Cooper's *Sea Lions*, Hawthorne's *Mosses from an Old Manse*, Francis Parkman's *California and Oregon Trail* – but he ultimately decided against reviewing books. As he said in another letter to Duyckinck, "In a little notice of *The Oregon Trail* I once said something 'critical' about another man's book – I shall never do it again. Hereafter I shall no more stab at a book (in print, I mean) than I would stab at a man" (*W*, XIV, p. 149). Not only did Melville find critiquing the work of others distasteful, he also found it difficult to switch off his brain and keep his reviews within their traditional bounds. Reading the work of others, he recognized where they could have taken their work but did not. He wanted to dive deeper.

Even in this friendly letter, Melville could not help but extend Hawthorne's ideas. Following his general view of *The House of the Seven Gables* with a brief discussion of the Clifford character, Melville launched a manifesto on the absolute. He imagined a man who could see the "absolute condition of present things" without fear, "the man who, like Russia or the British Empire, declares himself a sovereign nature (in himself) amid the powers of heaven, hell, and earth. He may perish; but so long as he exists he insists upon treating with all Powers upon an equal basis. If any of those other Powers choose to withhold certain secrets, let them; that does not impair my sovereignty in myself; that does not make me tributary" (*W*, XIV, p. 186). Tellingly, Melville shifts from the third person to the first in this passage. Hard at work on *Moby-Dick* when he wrote this letter, he began recognizing himself as the man who could see the absolute.

Much as he had with Duyckinck, Melville saw his correspondence with Hawthorne as a private form of writing intended only for each other's eyes. After his diatribe on the absolute, Melville explained, "You see, I began with a little criticism extracted for your benefit from the 'Pittsfield Secret Review,' and here I have landed in Africa" (*W*, XIV, p. 187). Describing his foray into literary criticism as an extract from a secret magazine, Melville privileged such private comments over those that appeared in the public press. No author could speak the absolute truth in a published work, but writing a confidential letter to a kindred spirit, Melville was free to speak his mind.

To another kindred spirit, Richard Henry Dana, Jr, Melville made a similar comment during the composition of *Moby-Dick*: "I almost think, I should hereafter – in the case of a sea book – get my M.S.S. neatly and legibly copied by a scrivener – send you that one copy – and deem such a procedure the best publication" (*W*, XIV, p. 160). After the commercial disappointment of *Mardi* and the artistic compromises he made with *Redburn* and *White-Jacket*, Melville had developed a genuine distaste for publishing. His comments to Hawthorne and Dana suggest that he would rather not publish at all. It would be better to keep his works in manuscript and share them with the few friends who could appreciate them. In manuscript, Melville could say what he could not say in print.

Upon the publication of *Moby-Dick*, Melville presented a copy of the book to Hawthorne, the dedicatee. Hawthorne enjoyed the book, dedication and all, and told Melville so in a heartfelt letter. The fact that he read and understood *Moby-Dick* thrilled Melville, who wished to keep Hawthorne's appreciation as a personal memento. He did not want to share it with anyone else. He wrote to Hawthorne to express his gratitude, but cautioned him against reviewing *Moby-Dick*: "Don't write a word about the book. That would be robbing me of my miserly delight. I am heartily sorry I ever wrote anything about you – it was paltry" (*W*, XIV, p. 213).

Mentioning something he had written about Hawthorne, Melville was referring specifically to "Hawthorne and his Mosses," the review-essay he had published in the *Literary World* the previous year. It may seem strange for Melville to regret this essay, since it was the single finest appreciation of Hawthorne published in his lifetime. The dichotomy between the public and the private implicit in so many of Melville's letters helps explain why he regretted "Hawthorne and His Mosses" and why he asked Hawthorne not to review *Moby-Dick*. The friendship and admiration they had developed for one another in person and through their correspondence was so special that Melville did not want to share it with anyone else, especially not the dull and insensitive reading public.

He reinforced their personal camaraderie in a postscript. He imagined having a paper mill established at one end of his house, which would supply "an endless riband of foolscap" upon which he would "write a thousand – a million – billion thoughts, all under the form of a letter to you. The divine magnet is in you, and my magnet responds. Which is the biggest? A foolish question – they are *One*" (*W*, XIX, p. 213). Hawthorne was his ideal reader, one who responded to his prose as a magnet.

Melville's desire to write a thousand billion thoughts also reflects the profound sense of energetic creativity he was experiencing at a time when *Moby-Dick* was finished and *Pierre* begun. The idea of putting these thousand billion thoughts into a private letter to Hawthorne instead of into a published book reveals his skepticism toward the literary marketplace. From Melville's point of view, a private letter to a kindred spirit let him do what a published book did not: to speak the truth and to be read, understood, and appreciated.

Rewriting history: *Israel Potter* and "Benito Cereno"

Though Melville had made liberal use of source material since becoming a writer, never had he based an individual work on a single printed source until he began writing for the magazines in the mid-1850s. Two works he serialized in *Putnam's* were each based on true stories published decades earlier. *Israel Potter* was based on *Life and Remarkable Adventures of Israel R. Potter* (1824), the personal story of an American Revolutionary patriot exiled in London for decades. "Benito Cereno" was based on a chapter from Amasa Delano's *Narrative of Voyages and Travels, in the Northern and Southern Hemispheres: Comprising Three Voyages Round the World* (1817). Relying on these texts for the basic plot of these two stories, Melville felt free to embellish his source material to make them more thrilling and more relevant for readers of the 1850s. To see how he departed from his sources is to watch his creative process unfold. Manipulating both narratives, Melville greatly enhanced the drama of each.

Israel Potter tells the story of an American who participates in the Battle of Bunker Hill, is made prisoner of war and brought to England, escapes from captivity, works for King George III at Kew Gardens, befriends some English sympathizers, goes on a secret mission to Paris, meets Benjamin Franklin, serves with John Paul Jones, sees Ethan Allen, and gets stranded in London in abject poverty for decades before returning to America. "Benito Cereno" depicts the aftermath of a slave revolt aboard the *San Dominick*, the Spanish slave ship Captain Delano unwittingly encounters in the harbor of Santa Maria, an island off the coast of Chile. Delano recognizes that the *San Dominick* is in trouble, comes to its rescue, and spends considerable time with Don Benito

Cereno without realizing the slaves aboard have taken control of the vessel. *Israel Potter* is more significant in terms of the historical events it concerns; "Benito Cereno" has greater resonance in terms of its ongoing political and social ramifications.

"Benito Cereno" surpasses *Israel Potter* in terms of literary quality, too. Listing the fifteen finest short stories in world literature, Edward O'Brien put "Benito Cereno" first, observing, "I regard this as the noblest short story in American literature. The balance of forces is complete, the atmosphere one of epic significance, the light cast upon the hero intense to the highest degree, the realization of the human souls profound, and the telling of the story orchestrated like a great symphony."[24] "Benito Cereno" excels partly because of its narrative point of view. Melville's use of the third-person narrator in *Israel Potter* is fairly conservative; "Benito Cereno" marks new advances in narrative technique.

From *Typee* through *White-Jacket*, Melville's narrative point of view remained fairly consistent. His first five books are all first-person narratives told by a narrator who closely resembles Melville himself. So is *Moby-Dick*, but Melville experimented more fully with the first-person narrative in his greatest book. Discussing Melville's narrative technique in *Moby-Dick*, John Huston observed, "It isn't just one man and one point of view – it is a half dozen men and different points of view. It is the writer, the moralist, the philosopher, the scientist, the cetologist, the dramatist."[25] Individual chapters experiment with different narrative approaches. Chapter 54, "The Town-Ho's Story," makes sophisticated use of the frame tale. And in "The Doubloon," Ishmael allows other members of the crew to take over the narration.

Pierre represents Melville's first extended effort with the third-person omniscient point of view, but he accomplished some extraordinary effects with it. The narrator of *Pierre* displays great depth of personality. *Pierre* is dedicated to Mt Greylock, which Melville could see from his study window at Arrowhead. Sometimes the narrator directly addresses the mountain. Attempting to explain the emotions stirring within his hero, he uses two different figures of speech – personification and apostrophe – imploring his mountain majesty to free him from the demands of truth: "Save me from being bound to Truth, liege lord, as I am now. How shall I steal yet further into Pierre, and show how this heavenly fire was helped to be contained in him, by mere contingent things, and things that he knew not. But I shall follow the endless, winding way, – the flowing river in the cave of man; careless whither I be led, reckless where I land" (*W*, VII, p. 107). The narrator of *Pierre* is unafraid to admit his uncertainties, unabashed to confess the difficulties he is having as he tries to articulate what Pierre felt deep within his heart.

When he began writing for the magazines, Melville reverted to the first person. The three earliest stories he composed were "Cock-A-Doodle-Doo!," "The Happy Failure," and "The Fiddler" (*W*, IX, p. 492). Though none were sailing narratives, all three were tales told by narrators not dissimilar to Melville himself. The last two were veiled retellings of the frustrations he had experienced within the literary marketplace. "Bartleby, the Scrivener," the next short story Melville composed, differs from the three earlier ones because the narrator, an old conservative lawyer, differs greatly from Melville himself. "Bartleby" exemplifies his increasingly sophisticated use of narrative point of view.

Melville's sources for both *Israel Potter* and "Benito Cereno" were first-person narratives, yet he chose to rewrite them in the third person. The change in point of view lets his narrators comment on events that happened in the past from the perspective of the present. The shift transforms the story of Israel Potter from reminiscence to retrospective. "Benito Cereno" transforms Amasa Delano's personal narrative into a modern commentary on the practice of slavery.

The third-person narrator in *Israel Potter* avoids the extravagances of *Pierre*'s narrator. Writing a historical romance filled with thrilling naval warfare, Melville used a narrative point of view not dissimilar to that of James Fenimore Cooper, the foremost author of historical romance and thrilling naval warfare in American literature. Unlike the narrator in *Pierre*, the narrator of *Israel Potter* seldom comments on the process of storytelling or articulates the difficulties he is experiencing as he tries to tell the story. He is the most conventional narrator Melville ever used in his work, a straightforward third-person omniscient narrator.

Israel Potter does contain some delightful narrative moments, however. In a chapter devoted to Benjamin Franklin, Israel enters a room where Franklin is seated. A long and humorous description of the great man's personal appearance follows. The narrator follows this elaborate description with a one-sentence paragraph: "But when Israel stepped within the chamber, he lost the complete effect of all this; for the sage's back, not his face, was turned to him" (*W*, VIII, p. 39). In other words, only after the description are we told that the picture of Franklin was not as he appeared to Israel but as he appears to the omniscient narrator. In this instance, the narrator is celebrating, even glorying in his omniscience. He, and only he, can view Franklin from all sides simultaneously.

In the following chapter, the narrator comments on his efforts to depict Franklin within the private realm rather than in the public sphere: "Seeking here to depict him in his less exalted habitudes, the narrator feels more as if he were playing with one of the sage's worsted hose, than reverentially handling the honored hat which once oracularly sat upon his brow" (*W*, VIII, p. 48). Though Melville took many liberties as he rewrote the story of Israel Potter, he assumed an overall narrative stance not dissimilar to that of the historian, who achieves objectivity by distancing himself from the events described. In this passage, Melville created further narrative distance by having the narrator refer to himself in the third person. Even as he distances himself, the narrator paradoxically shortens the distance between himself and his subject through the use of homey diction and imagery.

The objective viewpoint lets the narrator of *Israel Potter* speak with authority and make resounding pronouncements. Describing John Paul Jones shortly before the most dramatic episode in the book, the exciting naval battle between the *Bon Homme Richard* and the *Serapis*, the narrator finds Jones to be absolutely representative of his nation: "Intrepid, unprincipled, reckless, predatory, with boundless ambition, civilized in externals but a savage at heart, America is, or may yet be, the Paul Jones of nations" (*W*, VIII, p. 120). The narrator's objectivity reinforces the impact of this statement and reveals Melville's prescience.

With "Benito Cereno," Melville was doing essentially what he did with *Israel Potter*, that is, retelling an episode from history, but he experimented with narrative point of view more fully than he had in *Israel Potter*. The third-person narrator of "Benito Cereno," like the one in *Pierre*, takes on a distinct personality all his own. Unlike the one in *Pierre*, this narrator does not necessarily resemble Melville. Compared to other narrative personae Melville assumed over his career, the narrator of "Benito Cereno" comes closest to the "Virginian Spending July in Vermont," the persona Melville adopted for the anonymously published "Hawthorne and his Mosses."

Also published anonymously, "Benito Cereno" seems written by a Virginian or a Southerner or, at least, someone who accepts the racial stereotypes prevalent in the antebellum South. Describing Babo, the leader of the slave revolt who has assumed the role of personal servant to Benito Cereno to dupe Captain Delano, the narrator makes some comments about Blacks in general. He asserts that the Black has gained "the repute of making the most pleasing body servant in the world; one, too, whom a master need be on no stiffly superior terms with, but may treat with familiar trust; less a servant than a devoted companion" (*W*, IX, p. 52). These words do not reflect Melville's attitude toward Blacks; they are the words of a deliberately crafted narrative persona.

"Benito Cereno" echoes the rhetoric of the plantation novels that were in vogue in antebellum America at the time. John Pendleton Kennedy's *Swallow Barn*, to name the most important and well-known plantation novel, had appeared in a second edition around the same time *Moby-Dick* was published (and had received better reviews). In "Benito Cereno," Melville assumed a perspective similar to the plantation novels but for a different purpose. Whereas the plantation novels justified the practice of slavery, Melville turned the words of the plantation novelists around to reveal how insidious the practice of slavery could be. Overall, he tackled the problem of slavery with a delicate touch. Nowhere preachy or condemnatory, Melville rejected abolitionist rhetoric. Instead, he depicted the evils of slavery through the gradual accumulation of imaginative detail.

Composing the first part of "Benito Cereno," Melville took Amasa Delano's weather report – "light airs from the north east, and thick foggy weather" – and turned it into a moody and evocative passage:

> The morning was one peculiar to that coast. Everything was mute and calm; everything gray. The sea, though undulated into long roods of swells, seemed fixed, and was sleeked at the surface like waved lead that has cooled and set in the smelter's mould. The sky seemed a gray surtout. Flights of troubled gray fowl, kith and kin with flights of troubled gray vapors among which they were mixed, skimmed low and fitfully over the waters, as swallows over meadows before storms. Shadows present, foreshadowing deeper shadows to come.   (*W*, IX, pp. 812, 46)

This poetic description identifies "Benito Cereno" as a highly crafted literary work. As A. R. Humphreys noticed, it anticipates Joseph Conrad's depiction of Golfo Placido in *Nostromo*.[26] Melville effectively prepared his readers to pay attention as they read and keep an eye out for subtle nuances in the text. The passage also indicates the narrator's voice *before* he starts articulating Captain Delano's thoughts. Furthermore, this passage emphasizes the narrator's omniscience and his craftiness. He knows what is coming, but he is not going to reveal everything at once. The literary quality of this passage provides a standard for readers to use while perusing the rest of the narrative. Often, a highly wrought phrase or a literary allusion is the only clue to indicate that the narrator has resumed his own voice after speaking for Delano.

Describing Delano's initial reaction to what he sees aboard the *San Dominick*, the narrator imagines what Delano is thinking, modifying his conjecture with the word "perhaps." As the story proceeds, however, the narrator expresses precisely what Delano is thinking and closely identifies with him. The story's narrative complexity stems from Melville's use of focalization, a technique that allows a third-person narrator to convey the perspective of individual characters within the narrative. In the case of "Benito Cereno," the focalization oscillates between the narrator and Delano. The narrator frequently shrugs off his omniscience to see things as Delano sees them.

Focalizing the narration from Delano's perspective, Melville allowed his readers to learn what has happened aboard the *San Dominick* only as Delano learns what has happened. The perspective contributes greatly to the narrative's effectiveness, as contemporary reviewers recognized. One said that while reading "Benito Cereno" he "became nervously anxious for the solution of the mystery it involves." Another called it "a thrilling, weird-like narrative, which, read at midnight, gives an uncomfortable feeling to a powerful imagination." Yet another called it "a narrative that one reads with the same creeping horror which is experienced in perusing Coleridge's *Ancient Mariner*" (*CR*, pp. 482, 472–473). Clearly, Melville's narrative strategy worked. The possibility of a slave rebellion horrified many Americans in the 1850s.

To denote what Delano is thinking, the narrator uses three different techniques. Sometimes he puts Delano's thoughts in quotation marks. Other times he uses a tag clause, such as "thought Captain Delano." Yet other times, he does nothing to demarcate Delano's thoughts. He simply shifts from his own voice to articulate what Delano is thinking without giving the reader notice, a narrative technique known as free indirect discourse.

In the following passage, for example, the narrator speaks in the third person but takes Delano's perspective. Before it ends, the narrative shades into free indirect discourse. The narrator is describing how Delano looks at Benito Cereno's face and tries to interpret his personality: "Glancing over once more towards his host – whose side-face, revealed above the skylight, was now turned towards him – he was struck by the profile, whose clearness of cut was refined by the thinness incident to ill-health, as well as ennobled about the chin by the beard. Away with suspicion. He was a true off-shoot of a true hidalgo Cereno" (*W*, IX, p. 65). The second-to-last sentence – "Away with suspicion" – expresses what Delano was thinking without denoting it as such. His voice and the narrator's almost blend together as one. As the story progresses, Melville increasingly abandoned the use of both quotation marks and tag clauses, blurring the narrator's voice with Delano's. Sometimes it is unclear whose thoughts are being articulated.

The shaving episode – one of the great moments in American literature – offers a case in point. When Babo insists on giving Benito Cereno a shave, Cereno must endure his captor holding a sharp razor to his throat. As he watches the two men, Delano senses trouble but remains oblivious to what is really happening. One paragraph in this episode begins, "There is something in the negro which, in a peculiar way, fits him for avocations about one's person. Most negroes are natural valets and hairdressers; taking to the comb and brush congenially as to the castinets, and flourishing them apparently with almost equal satisfaction" (*W*, IX, p. 83). Whose thoughts are these? Are these Delano's thoughts expressed in the form of free indirect discourse? Or do they articulate what the narrator is thinking? Most readers have interpreted them as Delano's, but the complementary references to Samuel Johnson and Lord Byron hard by are undoubtedly the narrator's.

Either possibility is problematic. If these words are the narrator's, they suggest that by rewriting history, we impose our own prejudices onto the past. If they are Delano's, they suggest that history perpetuates the prejudices of the past into the present. Melville has trapped us – but he is not finished yet. Late in the tale he offers a different version of the story, this time told from Benito Cereno's perspective.

The final third of the work contains Benito Cereno's deposition, which fills in details Delano never knew or never realized. Some readers have found that the deposition detracts from the story as a whole. G. W. Curtis, who advised the editor of *Putnam's Magazine* to publish "Benito Cereno," enjoyed it very much but regretted Melville's ending: "It is a great pity he did not work it up as a connected tale instead of putting in the dreary documents at the end." In a follow-up letter, Curtis reiterated, "I should alter all the dreadful statistics at the end. Oh! dear, why can't Americans write good stories. They tell good lies enough, and plenty of 'em" (*Log*, II, pp. 500–504).

Curtis assumed Melville had taken the documents from his source, but Melville meticulously revised his source materials. He changed many minor details to enhance their literary quality. One slave, for example, is identified in Delano's original deposition as a caulker by trade. Melville changed caulker to gravedigger, giving the slave an occupation with much greater symbolic resonance. The original deposition describes the slaves' weaponry as "sticks and dagger." Melville revised the phrase to "hand-spikes and hatchets," thus using multiple literary devices – alliteration, assonance, and rhythm – to enhance the description (*W*, IX, pp. 104–105, 828). Most importantly, the character of Babo is a composite of three different men in the original deposition.

Melville's careful revisions contribute significantly to the story's sophistication. Whereas the main body of "Benito Cereno" is a third-person narrative that frequently articulates Delano's thoughts, the deposition, by its very nature, is a narrative told in the third person that articulates the perspective of the person giving the deposition. Including the deposition, Melville allowed himself the opportunity to retell the story all over again from a different perspective. Structurally "Benito Cereno" recalls Poe's detective stories. "The Purloined Letter," for example, splits into two parts, the first part telling a dramatic mystery and the second part explaining how the detective solved the mystery. The first two thirds of "Benito Cereno" tell a tension-filled story; the deposition allows Benito Cereno to explain precisely what had happened.

While the deposition retells the story from a second perspective, it also begs a question: why didn't Melville retell it from a third? The story is never related from Babo's perspective. Being omniscient, the narrator could have articulated Babo's viewpoint, too – but he could not have done so and maintained the story's dramatic tensions. Arguably, Babo is the tale's original teller: he is the one who instigated the uprising that provides the story's drama. He is the one who created the fiction that duped Captain Delano while aboard the *San Dominick*. And he, the Black, is the one history has silenced.

Modern man: "The Lightning-Rod Man," *The Confidence-Man*, "Bartleby, the Scrivener"

In Melville's writings, the theme of modernity occurs at least as early as *White-Jacket*. Thinking about the attitude of sailors aboard a man-of-war, White Jacket considers the link between occupation and temperament: "A forced, interior quietude, in the midst of great outward commotion, breeds moody people. Who so moody as rail-road-brakemen, steam-boat engineers, helmsmen, and tenders of power-looms in cotton factories? For all these must hold their peace while employed, and let the machinery do the chatting; they can not even edge in a single syllable" (*W*, V, p. 46). White Jacket's observation addresses two particular elements of modernity: machines and the noises they make. Since the clatter of machinery prevents speech, their operators must keep whatever they wish to say bottled up inside themselves. Denied an outlet for expression, those who operate machines have nowhere to turn. The machine is their muzzle and their prison.

Man's place in the modern world is just one of many themes touched upon in the grab bag of ideas that is *White-Jacket*. Virtually every work Melville wrote afterwards broaches this theme to a greater or lesser extent. In some of his later works, he made the theme of modernity central: "The Lightning-Rod Man," *The Confidence-Man*, and "Bartleby, the Scrivener." The title characters of all three works represent different aspects of modernity.

The Lightning-Rod Man symbolizes the materialism that was becoming an increasingly important aspect of American culture during the mid-nineteenth century. His story belongs to a popular genre of magazine tale known as the salesman story. Typically, salesman stories tell the adventures of Yankee peddlers traveling around the countryside selling their wares.[27] As a door-to-door salesman, the Lightning-Rod Man represents the world of getting and spending at its crassest level. His business has given him a paranoia symptomatic of modern times. He takes every precaution he can to guard against lightning.

As he explains to the narrator, a householder he has imposed upon: "I avoid pine-trees, high houses, lonely barns, upland pastures, running water, flocks of cattle and sheep, a crowd of men" (*W*, IX, p. 123). His business has so affected his mind that the Lightning-Rod Man has completely disassociated himself from nature, from the agrarian ideal, and from his fellow man. His business has consumed him to such an extent that he can think of nothing else.

The narrator's complacency contrasts sharply with the salesman's paranoia. The story begins prior to the Lightning-Rod Man's arrival. The narrator is enjoying the sight and sound of a thunderstorm from his cozy mountain home. Hearing the awesome thunder and seeing the sublime lightning, he decides that the mountains must churn up the thunderstorms and make them more glorious than they are on the plains. The narrator of "The Lightning-Rod Man" is the human equivalent of the Catskill eagle in *Moby-Dick*. He lives in a low house, but his house is in the mountains and therefore closer to the heavens. A knock on the door heralds the Lightning-Rod Man and disturbs the householder's enjoyment of the storm. Being a good host, he invites the peddler indoors and listens to his spiel. Reaching the point where he usually clinches the deal, the salesman provokes the narrator's ire instead. His description of what happens to a person who has been struck by lightning is especially offensive: "Think of being a heap of charred offal, like a haltered horse burnt in his stall; – and all in one flash!" (*W*, IX, p. 124).

These graphic words eliminate the sense of the storm's awe and grandeur the narrator had been enjoying earlier. In place of sublime beauty, the salesman has substituted a gruesome image of personal destruction. The narrator is a romantic, the salesman a realist. Having lost touch with nature, the salesman has lost touch with what is grand in nature. Like Ossian, the legendary Gaelic poet, the narrator imagines the sound of rain as part of an epic battle. The pelting of the pitiless storm resembles "a charge of spear-points." Alternatively, the salesman hears the storm and can only foresee his transformation into "a heap of charred offal." Refusing to debase his imagination, the narrator grabs the sample lightning rod the salesman is holding, bends it in two, and drags the salesman out the door.

Tossing the Lightning-Rod Man from his home, the narrator triumphs over him. In symbolic terms, the realm of the imagination has triumphed over the world of business. The narrator's personal victory over the Lightning-Rod Man is an isolated incident, however. Elsewhere in the neighborhood, the salesman experiences resounding success. Though the narrator has cautioned his neighbors against him, the Lightning-Rod Man "still travels in storm-time, and drives a brave trade with the fears of man" (*W*, IX, pp. 124). The community comes over to the salesman's way of thinking. In his resistance to modern technology and dislike of modern techniques of salesmanship, the narrator is isolated from his community. The fundamental options the Lightning-Rod Man offers the narrator are bleak: conformity or isolation.

Seeing the Lightning-Rod Man as a harbinger of modern times is just one possible interpretation of his character. He has also been seen as an evangelist preacher seeking converts. Q. D. Leavis found him a combination of Calvinist minister, Catholic priest, hellfire religionist, missionary, and witch doctor.[28] Great literature lends itself to multiple interpretations simultaneously, and other interpretations are possible. The salesman's effort to get the narrator's name down on his list resembles the traditional behavior of the devil. The fact that Melville took attributes associated with the devil and assigned them to a character whose behavior resembles an itinerant preacher enhances his satirical depiction of evangelical Christianity. Giving preacherly attributes to a Yankee peddler, Melville paralleled religion with commercialism. Advocates of either try to sell us things we do not need.

The Lightning-Rod Man anticipates the behavior of another Melville character, the Confidence Man, who also manifests the traditional behavior of the devil. Not only does the Confidence Man carry out the devil's desire to get people to sign their names in his book, he also has the ability to change shapes at will, another attribute of the devil common to folk legend. Though the Confidence Man exemplifies centuries-old devil lore, he also reflects a new development in modern American culture. The term "confidence man" had only entered the English language a decade or so before *The Confidence-Man* appeared in 1856. Melville recognized a profound similarity between the legendary devil and the modern confidence man. Both succeed in their efforts because they appeal to greed and take advantage of naiveté.

Setting *The Confidence-Man* aboard a Mississippi riverboat, Melville gave his title character a distinct advantage over the people he tries to gull. Unlike the householder who narrates "The Lightning-Rod Man," they are rootless. They have no attachments and thus are more vulnerable to the Confidence Man's spiel. Furthermore, the passengers aboard lack the presence of mind the narrator of "The Lightning-Rod Man" possesses. They are the equivalent of the neighbors mentioned toward the end of that story. With few strong convictions of their own they succumb to the smooth talk of a seductive stranger.

The Confidence-Man allowed Melville to continue exploring the relationship between appearance and reality. Because they can assume different identities to swindle their victims, con artists thrive within the anonymity of the modern world. They prey upon people's desire for human contact and take advantage of those who naively assume that they can judge people by their appearance.

Reading *The Confidence-Man* requires close concentration. In its early chapters, the title character changes identity often. In the third chapter, for example, he appears as Black Guinea, a crippled man who plays a tambourine and catches pennies in his mouth. His strange appearance and unusual activity attracts a crowd of onlookers. When one member of the crowd questions his handicap, Black Guinea lists several references. His list provides a clue to the book as a whole: it names a number of the guises in which the Confidence Man will appear. By the "gemmen wid a brass plate," for example, Black Guinea refers to the agent from the Philosophical Intelligence Office, who wears a brass badge engraved "P.I.O." Once the third chapter gives way to the fourth, Black Guinea has disappeared, and the Confidence Man has assumed a new identity.

In his guise as the agent from the Philosophical Intelligence Office, the Confidence Man provides a good indication of his typical behavior. He behaves somewhat differently from modern-day con artists. After baiting their intended victims with potential rewards, con artists typically stroke their victims, giving them feelings of happiness, success, and well-being. Though Melville's Confidence Man baits his victims, he usually avoids stroking them. Instead of telling them what they want to hear and making them feel good about themselves, he challenges their prejudices and preconceptions and makes them uneasy.[29] Posing as a man from an intelligence office or, in modern parlance, an employment agency, the Confidence Man selects as his victim a Missouri bachelor who calls himself Pitch. The encounter with Pitch provides a good indication of the Confidence Man's behavior as a whole. Aware of Pitch's prejudice against hired hands, the Confidence Man deliberately chooses a difficult con. He will try to get Pitch to do something he does not want to do, to hire a boy to help him work the farm.

The best con artists can size up their victims quickly. The Missouri bachelor is an easy read. Pitch is "somewhat ursine in aspect; sporting a shaggy spencer of the cloth called bear's-skin; a high-peaked cap of raccoon-skin, the long bushy tail switching over behind; rawhide leggings; grim stubble chin; and to end, a double-barreled gun in hand" (*W*, X, p. 106). In other words, the Missouri bachelor is the stereotypical American frontiersman. According to type, he is a rugged individualist, a man whose gun can get him what he needs to survive – clothing, food, shelter. He closely resembles Jim Doggett, the Arkansas hunter in Thomas Bangs Thorpe's classic short story, "The Big Bear of Arkansas." Published a decade and a half earlier and set on a Mississippi riverboat, Thorpe's tale anticipates *The Confidence-Man* in many ways. J. A. Leo Lemay reads "The Big Bear of Arkansas" as an elegy for the American frontier; by the time *The Confidence-Man* appeared a decade and a half later, the frontier had virtually disappeared.[30] The Missouri bachelor is no longer able to remain in the backwoods and fend for himself. He has taken to farming. Self-reliance has gone by the wayside. Unable to work his farm alone, he has been forced to hire boys to help him.

Dissatisfied with the lazy, conniving, insolent boys he has hired so far, Pitch now puts his faith in machines. He rebuffs the Confidence Man's initial effort to persuade him to hire another boy. "Machines for me," he tells the Confidence Man. "My cider-mill – does that ever steal my cider? My mowing-machine – does that ever lay a-bed mornings? My corn-husker – does that ever give me insolence? No: cider-mill, mowing-machine, corn-husker – all faithfully attend to their business." The Missouri bachelor predicts that man as a working animal is almost extinct:

> I say, that boy or man, the human animal is, for most work-purposes, a losing animal. Can't be trusted; less trustworthy than oxen; for conscientiousness a turn-spit dog excels him. Hence these thousand new inventions – carding machines, horse-shoe machines, tunnel-boring machines, reaping machines, apple-paring machines, boot-blacking machines, sewing machines, shaving machines, run-of-errand machines, dumb-waiter machines, and the Lord only knows what machines; all of which announce the era when that refractory animal, the working or serving man, shall be a buried by-gone, a superseded fossil.   (*W*, X, p. 117)

The Missouri bachelor's mind seems made up, but the Confidence Man, successfully challenging his prejudices, finally persuades him to hire yet another boy. The Missouri bachelor pays the boy's salary in advance and even gives the Confidence Man the boy's passage money. In the next chapter the agent from the Philosophical Intelligence Office is nowhere in sight, and Pitch realizes he has been taken. He guards against being swindled again, hardening his heart toward all mankind. When the Confidence Man approaches him in his guise as the Cosmopolitan, Pitch refuses to trust him at all.

With the character of the Missouri bachelor, Melville captured mankind at a perilous moment. The rugged individualism that the American frontiersman symbolized was disappearing with the frontier. Individuals now need help to survive, but, paradoxically, modern times alienates man from fellow man. The case of the Missouri bachelor suggests that man has only two options, to live in an increasingly impersonal, mechanized world or to put trust in others. After trusting the Confidence Man and being swindled, Pitch becomes a thoroughgoing misanthrope. His contact with the Confidence Man ultimately isolates him from all men.

"Bartleby, the Scrivener" also takes man's alienation, isolation, and unknowability as major themes. The story begins with a traditional motif – the arrival of a mysterious stranger – but over its course it becomes a parable for modern times. Melville's "Bartleby" is reminiscent of Balzac's *Colonel Chabert*. Balzac used the same motif and a similar setting – a mysterious stranger entering a lawyer's office – but the two title characters have opposite reasons for wanting to see a lawyer. Colonel Chabert seeks the restoration of his family name; Bartleby seeks the anonymity that comes with menial labor.[31] Bartleby is defined by the job he takes. Assuming his role as scrivener, he loses whatever hold on individuality he formerly had.

The urban setting of "Bartleby" emphasizes the story's modernity. Set in Wall Street, where the pulse of the nation is measured by the flow of money, the story of Bartleby occurs in an increasingly impersonal and unnatural place. The old lawyer who hires Bartleby and subsequently tells his story, has remained in the same office while tall buildings have been erected around him. Bartleby's desk gives him an unobstructed view of a brick wall. His physical situation reflects his psychological state. Working in an office surrounded by tall buildings, he finds himself trapped, walled in by a life he dislikes. The old lawyer is initially satisfied with his work, but Bartleby's competence does nothing to dispel the lawyer's uneasiness. He explains, "I should have been quite delighted with his application, had he been cheerfully industrious. But he wrote on silently, palely, mechanically" (*W*, IX, pp. 19–20).

Working like a machine, Bartleby has become part of the increasingly mechanized, modernized, regularized world. His story anticipates King Vidor's *The Crowd* and other films that depict man's increasingly insignificant place in the modern world. Jonathan Parker's *Bartleby*, which may be the finest film adaptation of any Melville work, shows how easily the story translates to the twenty-first century. Bartleby is an everyman for modern times. Writing in the mid-twentieth century, C. L. R. James found that Bartleby foreshadowed "those millions of human beings who spend their strength, vitality and capacity for living, day after day, taking down, typing, checking, filing and then looking for documents which are to them as dead as the dead letters Bartleby handled."[32]

Bartleby ultimately does something no machine can do, however. He exerts his will. Like the hero in Ivan Goncharov's *Oblomov*, Bartleby takes action in the form of passivity. One day when the lawyer asks him to perform one of the typical duties of a scrivener, Bartleby first articulates his catch phrase, words of quiet yet unmistakable defiance: "I would prefer not to." His words become increasingly frequent during the course of the story until he reaches the point where he refuses all work. When the lawyer tries to get him to leave, he prefers not to. In its inexorability, Bartleby's defiant phrase becomes the mantra of a man waiting for death.

Battle-Pieces: the voices of war

The prose supplement Melville appended to *Battle-Pieces and Aspects of War* begins, "Were I fastidiously anxious for the symmetry of this book, it would close with the notes. But the times are such that patriotism – not free from solicitude – urges a claim overriding all literary scruples" (*Works*, XIV, p. 180). While claiming to put patriotism above literary concerns, Melville's collection of verse retains a high level of symmetry, even with the supplement. The unusual layout of the first edition of *Battle-Pieces* suggests that he added a prefatory poem entitled "The Portent" *after* he wrote the supplement. Set entirely in italics, "The Portent" is not listed in the table of contents, and it appears on what seems originally intended as a blank leaf or a half-title page. This prefatory poem balances out the concluding supplement and enhances the book's overall symmetry. "The Portent" is set before the Civil War began; the supplement suggests what to do now that the war has ended.

In terms of its imagery and symbolic associations, "The Portent" provides a good indication of the poems that follow. The body of militant abolitionist John Brown hanging from the gallows forms its central image. One of the finest poems in the volume, "The Portent" is short enough to be quoted in full. Since Melville put much thought into the physical appearance of *Battle-Pieces*, any quotation from it should retain its typographical eccentricities, italics in the case of "The Portent":

> *Hanging from the beam,*
>   *Slowly swaying (such the law),*
> *Gaunt the shadow on your green,*
>   *Shenandoah!*
> *The cut is on the crown*
> *(Lo, John Brown),*
> *And the stabs shall heal no more.*
>
> *Hidden in the cap*
>   *Is the anguish none can draw;*
> *So your future veils its face,*
>   *Shenandoah!*
> *But the streaming beard is shown*
> *(Weird John Brown),*
> *The meteor of the war.*
>   (*Works*, XVI, p. 5)

The body casts a dark shadow over the Shenandoah Valley in the first stanza. In the second, the speaker of the poem describes the hood that covers Brown's face and, consequently, masks whatever pain it reflects at the moment of death.

The speaker draws a parallel between Brown and the Shenandoah by using the word "face" figuratively to refer to the face of the countryside, which is doubly obscured by a shadow of a hooded man. The hood does not completely cover Brown's facial features; his long beard remains visible.

The physiognomist can use this one detail to interpret the meaning of Brown's face and the future of the Shenandoah. In Melville's day, a comet's tail was also called its beard. Instead of a comet, Melville decided a meteor would be more appropriate, in terms of the rise and fall of Brown's career as an abolitionist but also in terms of the traditional superstitions associated with meteors. Thoreau and Whitman also found the analogy appropriate: both men compared Brown to meteors in their writings.[33] Brown is weird like the Weird Sisters in *Macbeth*. He both influences and anticipates the future. A martyr in the abolitionist cause, John Brown, in death, foreshadows the battles that would occur and the blood that would be shed in the coming years.

The tone of voice Melville chose for "The Portent" looks forward to subsequent poems in *Battle-Pieces*. Many possess a similar melancholy. Published after the Civil War ended, *Battle-Pieces* retells events of the preceding six years, but the poems sound as if they are describing events from eons ago. Contemporary readers noticed this quality in them. Watts De Peyster, for one, quoted several lines from "Chattanooga" and thought they recalled "the far distant past." Depicting Ulysses S. Grant's assault on the Confederate stronghold atop Missionary Ridge in November 1863, "Chattanooga" reminded De Peyster of the dying words of Epaminondas, the leader of the Theban army.[34]

Reviewing *Battle-Pieces* for the *Atlantic*, William Dean Howells found in Melville's war poetry the "heroic quality of remoteness, separating our weak human feelings from them by trackless distances." Howells also identified Melville's literary model. "Lyon," a poem commemorating General Nathaniel Lyon, who fell in a battle to gain control of the Missouri River, Howells called "a bit as far off from us as any of Ossian's, but undeniably noble" (*CR*, pp. 527–528). Comparing *Battle-Pieces* to the poems of Ossian, Howells recognized an important source for Melville's melancholy and the faraway quality of his verse.

Written by James Macpherson and inspired by traditional Gaelic verse, the prose poems of Ossian were hugely popular during the late eighteenth and early nineteenth century. *Fingal, An Ancient Epic Poem*, one of Macpherson's Ossianic works, emphasizes the bard's importance on the battlefield. Fallen heroes need someone to sing their song, and Macpherson made the poet as essential to the battlefield as the warrior. In his copy of *Fingal*, Melville marked many passages that moved him. The following excerpt, which Melville partly underlined, provides a good indication of the Ossianic style: "O that thou wouldst come to my hall when I am alone by night! – And thou dost come, my friend, I hear often thy light hand on my harp; when it hangs on the distant wall, and the feeble sound touches my ear. Why dost thou not speak to me in my grief, and tell when I shall behold my friends! But thou passest away in thy murmuring blast; and thy wind whistles through the gray hair of Ossian." In the margin adjacent to this passage, Melville placed an X, a mark referring to a note he inscribed at the top of the page: "What can be finer than this? It is the soul of melancholy."[35]

In addition to borrowing their melancholy tone, Melville also took imagery from the poems of Ossian. Retelling the Battle of the Wilderness, which pitted Grant's Army of the Potomac against Robert E. Lee's Army of Northern Virginia, Melville alluded to "Carthon," one of the most popular Ossianic prose poems. In this work, Fingal laments how nature has reclaimed Balclutha, a walled town belonging to the Britons. In his copy of *Fingal*, Melville partly underlined the following passage: "I have seen the walls of Balclutha, but they were desolate. The fire had resounded in the halls; and the voice of the people is no more. The stream of Clutha was removed from its place, by the fall of the walls. – The thistle shook, there, its lonely head: the moss whistled to the wind. The fox looked out, from the windows, the rank grass of the wall waved round his head."[36] In "The armies of the Wilderness," Melville imagined how the deserted military camps would appear in the last days of the war, when few soldiers remained in the field besides Colonel John Mosby's Virginia guerillas:

> That eve a stir was in the camps,
>   Forerunning quiet soon to come
> Among the streets of beechen huts
>   No more to know the drum.
> The weed shall choke the lowly door,
>   And foxes peer within the gloom,
> Till scared perchance by Mosby's prowling men,
>   Who ride in the rear of doom.
>   (*Works*, XVI, p. 72)

The Ossianic voice is just one of many voices Melville used in *Battle-Pieces*. A brief introductory note prior to the table of contents explains that the poems are spoken from many different perspectives. In this note, Melville asserted that he drafted poems from various points of view without trying to maintain any sort of consistency. He compares his technique to an Aeolian harp, a favorite image of the Romantic poets: "I seem, in most of these verses, to have but placed a harp in a window, and noted the contrasted airs which wayward winds have played upon the strings" (*Works*, XVI, p. 3). The random quality Melville asserts is a pose, but some contemporary readers took his explanation at face value. One characterized *Battle-Pieces* as "a basket of poetical chips scored out at random, some showing good sound timber, and others a trifle punky."[37] Overall, the poems that comprise *Battle-Pieces* are unified by their subject matter and rough chronological organization. Melville's change of voices from one poem to the next adds variety and, as the subtitle suggests, allows him to depict many different aspects of war.

In two consecutive poems, he retold the story of the battle between the *Monitor* and the *Merrimac*. Each is told in a different voice. The speaker of "The Temeraire," a poem that takes Turner's painting of a great wooden warship as a point of comparison, is told by "an Englishman of the old order." The voice Melville chose for the subsequent poem is obvious from its title, "A Utilitarian View of the Monitor's Fight." With his short stories, Melville was fond of joining together two contrasting episodes into one. Placed adjacent to one another, these two poems function similarly. Each expressing ideas of their own, the two poems become more complex in juxtaposition.

"The Temeraire" laments the passing of the splendors of battle, the "garniture, emblazonment, / And heraldry." The speaker of the poem recalls great ships of the line and the exquisite craftsmanship these vessels displayed. As Melville's own notes explain, old cannons were "cast in shapes which Cellini might have designed, were gracefully enchased, generally with the arms of the country." The Englishman returns to Turner's painting toward the end, which depicts a pitiful image: "A pigmy steam-tug tows you, / Gigantic, to the shore" (*Works*, XVI, pp. 41, 174, 42).

"A Utilitarian View of the Monitor's Fight" attempts what seems an impossible task, to find a way to put modern warfare into verse. Traditional poetic diction will not work. The poet must find language that suits the practical nature of the latest armament and weaponry. The poem begins with the following stanza:

> Plain be the phrase, yet apt the verse,
> > More ponderous than nimble;
> For since grimed War here laid aside
> His Orient pomp, 'twould ill befit
> > Overmuch to ply
> The rhyme's barbaric cymbal.

While acknowledging the impropriety of traditional poetic technique, this opening stanza has yet to choose the appropriate language. By the third stanza, the poet had adopted the language of engineering to convey the battle: "No passion; all went on by crank, / Pivot, and screw, / And calculations of caloric" (*Works*, XVI, p. 44).

The different voices Melville used for these two poems present different aspects of the clash between the *Monitor* and the *Merrimac*, but neither attempt to retell the story of the battle. In "The Temeraire," the old Englishman sees this new kind of warfare with a sense of nostalgia. The speaker of "A Utilitarian View," while cognizant of poetic tradition, realizes that modern times call for a new approach to verse. How different all this is from what Melville had written the previous decade in *Israel Potter*. His depiction of the fight between the *Bon Homme Richard* and the *Serapis* in that book is one of the finest naval battles in American literature. Modern literature has no place for tales of glory in battle.

In "Donelson," a poem that describes the Southern surrender of Fort Donelson in Tennessee, Melville made imaginative use of typeface and punctuation to convey several different voices. The poem begins in roman type. The speaker of the poem, as Stanton Garner noticed, is not Melville but a dramatic character in the poem.[38] A group of interested citizens has gathered around the bulletin board of a newspaper office during an icy rainstorm to read the latest telegraphic news reports. A shorter member of the crowd calls out to a taller one to read the posted report aloud. The headline of the news report, set in small caps, follows, and the report itself is set in italics. The poem alternates between the narrator's description of the crowd gathered around the bulletin board day after day and the news reports that depict the action at Fort Donelson.

Describing Melville's technique in "Donelson," Hennig Cohen called it "almost cinematic."[39] Melville was using a technique that would become known as cross-cutting. Much as a filmmaker cuts between action that takes place at two different locations, Melville switches back and forth between the bulletin board and the battlefield. The close-up is another technique Melville used in "Donelson." After the tall man has finished reading the first bulletin and the crowd has dispersed, Melville inserted a poignant close-up of the posted bulletin: "Washed by the storm till the paper grew / Every shade of a streaky blue, / That bulletin stood" (*Works*, XVI, p. 23). This close-up puts a period to what had come before and serves as a transition for what follows. In "Donelson," Melville combines sound and image to tell the story of the fall of Fort Donelson but also to depict the production of news during wartime.

"Lee in the Capitol," the second to last poem in *Battle-Pieces*, depicts Robert E. Lee's appearance before Congress after the war. In this poem, Melville took the opportunity to try out other voices. The speaker of the poem resembles an ancient historian, who incorporates speeches from great leaders within his work. A note to the poem compares it with ancient histories as well as Shakespeare's historic plays. This poem also let Melville give the leader of the

Confederate Army a voice. Lee tells the senators that the North must take the responsibility of befriending the South:

> Shall the great North go Sylla's way?
> Proscribe? prolong the evil day?
> Confirm the curse? infix the hate?
> In Union's name forever alienate?
>   (*Works*, XVI, p. 167)

By "Sylla," Melville was referring to Sulla, the Roman leader who nonchalantly ordered the slaughter of thousands of Roman citizens – "a few rebels whom I have ordered to be chastised," he said. The reviewer for a leading Southern magazine recognized Melville's sympathy with the South and cited "Lee in the Capitol" for proof. This reviewer sensed in Melville "a secret misgiving, as to whether much that was done, was in reality justified by the laws of humanity which rise higher than those of war."[40]

In the prose supplement to *Battle-Pieces*, Melville dropped the personae he had used throughout the collection and spoke in his own voice. St Loe Strachey compared the supplement to Wordsworth's letter to Charles W. Pasley, in which Wordsworth eloquently disagreed with ideas about war Pasley articulated in his *Essay on the Military Policy of the Institutions of the British Empire*. After establishing his name as a poet, Wordsworth claimed the right to speak politically. With *Battle-Pieces*, Melville established his reputation as a poet. In the supplement, a political essay unlike anything he had ever written before, Melville, too, was claiming the right to speak politically. Through much of the essay, he argues for tolerance and reconciliation between North and South. In his closing paragraph, however, he retreats to the role of litterateur: "Let us pray that the terrible historic tragedy of our time may not have been enacted without instructing our whole beloved country through terror and pity; and may fulfilment verify in the end those expectations which kindle the bards of Progress and Humanity" (*Works*, XVI, p. 190). His diction echoes Aristotle's classic definition of tragedy.[41] He had begun by putting patriotism above literary scruples. His closing sentence reasserts his role as a poet. Unlike Ossian, however, he does not define himself as a bard of war, but rather as one of the "bards of Progress of Humanity."

Clarel, an American epic

Some of the finest poets in American literature have chosen the epic as their medium of expression. Tracing this phenomenon from Walt Whitman's *Song of Myself* to John Berryman's *Dream Songs*, Patrick White identified similarities between modern American verse and such epics as Milton's *Paradise Lost* and Homer's *Odyssey*.[42] White did not consider *Clarel*, but it belongs to the American epic tradition, too, as readers started recognizing upon its publication. Some have compared *Clarel* to other poems in the tradition. Richard Chase, for one, observed that the poem's imagery "will make the reader think that if *Clarel* were mercilessly compressed, it would sound a great deal like T. S. Eliot's *Waste Land*."[43] It's easy to call a poem an epic; it's something else to prove it. The criteria White used to analyze Berryman can be applied to Melville. *Clarel* contains all the requisite epic elements. It has the capacity to be an epic, and its hero bears attributes of the epic hero. As a pilgrimage, *Clarel* contains a small group of men who represent a greater community paralleling the communities defined by other epic poems. And *Clarel* possesses the dignity of an epic.

Epic capacity concerns the poem's overall scope. In terms of sheer size, *Clarel* seems long enough to qualify as an epic. In the standard edition of Melville's writings, it fills nearly five hundred pages. Melville divided *Clarel* into four roughly equal parts; each part is further subdivided into cantos. Part 1, "Jerusalem," introduces the title character, an American divinity student who has traveled to the Holy Land in hopes of quelling his growing doubts about religion. Tired of formal learning, Clarel has come to the desert to purge his soul of "bookish vapors" (*W*, XII, p. 5). In Jerusalem, he meets the characters who will accompany him on his pilgrimage and falls in love with a Jewish girl named Ruth, whose father is killed by Arab terrorists. In Part 2, "The Wilderness," Clarel and his fellow pilgrims travel from Jerusalem to the Dead Sea. The title of Part 3, "Mar Saba," refers to a fifth-century Greek monastery, which serves as the central setting for this part of the poem. Part 4, "Bethlehem," takes Clarel and the other surviving pilgrims to the place of Christ's nativity and returns them to Jerusalem, where he discovers that Ruth has died in his absence.

Length alone is insufficient to make a poem an epic. Epic poets have the responsibility to present what White called "the whole of life relative to their culture."[44] From the Renaissance to the modernist era, the center of the epic shifted from God to the poet-hero. Formerly, the whole of life embraced by an epic referred to spiritual life; now, it refers to the life of the poet. The whole of life in *Clarel* is neither God-centered nor self-centered. Rather, it bridges these two perspectives. *Clarel* effectively captures the shift in focus from God to self. Set in the Holy Land and imbued with religious history, it takes as its subject the clash between faith and skepticism that was reaching a crisis point during the second half of the nineteenth century.

Numerous examples from *Clarel* could be used to illustrate its epic capacity. Take "By Achor," the fourteenth canto of Part 2, for instance. This canto brings Clarel and his fellow pilgrims past the mountains of Moab, the range that included Mt Pisgah, where Moses stood to see the promised land. The sight of these mountains elicits a response from Mortmain, a Swede whose former idealism has been reduced to bleak despair. The character's name, which literally means "dead hand," is a legal term concerning how the dead could control property they left behind. Melville was not the first to make poetic use of the term. In "Haunted houses," Henry Wadsworth Longfellow wrote: "Owners and occupants of earlier dates / From graves forgotten stretch their dusty hands, / And hold in mortmain still their old estates."

In *Clarel*, Mortmain is both representative and harbinger of death, as his reaction to the mountains of Moab show. These mountains resonate with sacred history, but neither the sight of them nor their Biblical associations softens Mortmain's pessimism. As the pilgrims view the mountain range, clouds pass overhead, casting shadows over the land. Mortmain exclaims, "Lo, how they trail, / The mortcloths in the funeral / Of gods!" (*W*, XII, p. 178). Seeing this vista of mountain and valley, sunlight and shade, Mortmain, far from being inspired by the beauty of creation, interprets what he sees as a funeral procession. He is witnessing the death of religious belief.

Derwent, an Anglican priest whose cheery optimism masks the shallowness of his belief, is offended by the pessimistic comment, which destroys the scenic beauty for him and ruins his enjoyment of the Biblical terrain. The way Derwent characterizes what Mortmain has said brings into question his own ability to appreciate the true meaning of the sacred landmarks they encounter. Using a simile, Derwent compares Mortmain's words to "harsh grit in oiled machine." The comparison may sound unusual, but it is not as incomprehensible as J. R. Wise made it seem.[45] In essence, Derwent puts Moses in the machine age, unintentionally denigrating the sacred past by using a ready-made symbol of the modern age to interpret Biblical history. Glossing the passage, Walter Bezanson found Derwent's words thematically relevant to the poem as a whole, the force of modern technology being partly responsible for mankind's loss of faith (*W*, XII, pp. 178, 545).

Regardless of the differences between Mortmain and Derwent, their words illustrate the vast sweep of time and the broad outlook Melville's epic embodies. Though set in a land imbued with religious associations thousands of years old, *Clarel* refers to numerous aspects of modern culture. Throughout this long poem, Melville brings together the religious past and the secular present to see if both can coexist. Is religion still valid in the age of science and technology, an era when engineers, not priests, have assumed the responsibility for solving man's problems? Is sacred history relevant in the face of scientific fact? Tackling such issues, Melville created a poem with an almost limitless capacity. From pessimism to optimism, past to present, earth to heavens, man to God, *Clarel* ranges freely between the known and the unknown.

Every epic requires an epic hero. At first glance, Clarel might seem to lack sufficient stature to assume this role. But it is important to distinguish between the epic hero and the tragic hero. Clarel lacks the tragic grandeur of both Ahab and Pierre, but the epic hero need not possess grandeur; he need only symbolize it. As a representative of the United States and a manifestation of epistemological uncertainty – a dreamer and a doubter – Clarel stands for things and ideas greater than himself. As a representative national type whose behavior reflects American behavior at large, he takes on epic proportions. As a man in the making, he follows a long-standing tradition in American literature. His amorphous quality makes him an ideal hero to embody the uncertainty of modern times, too. Newton Arvin found Clarel a forerunner for the unassuming protagonists of modern fiction, such as Hans Castorp in Thomas Mann's great novel, *The Magic Mountain.*[46]

Clarel's malleability forms one of his defining characteristics. In his search for something to believe in, he keeps a watchful eye on his fellow pilgrims, observing them, listening to what they say, trying to understand their ideas and beliefs. In the first canto, Clarel is closely drawn to Vine, a shy character who keeps mostly to himself. Together, Clarel, Vine, and Rolfe visit a stone overlooking Jerusalem where, legend has it, Christ sat and prophesied the city's destruction. Rolfe describes the appearance of Jerusalem in relation to its past. While listening to Rolfe, Clarel looks at the shy and sensitive Vine and tries to interpret Rolfe's words based on the changes in Vine's physiognomy:

> Clarel gave ear, albeit his glance
> Diffident skimmed Vine's countenance,
> As mainly here he interest took
> In all the fervid speaker said,
> Reflected in the mute one's look:
> A face indeed quite overlaid
> With tremulous meanings, which evade
> Or shun regard, nay, hardly brook
> Fraternal scanning.
> (*W*, XII, p. 107)

The last phrase suggests that two kindred spirits should be able to discern what the other one thinks. Clarel's attempt to fathom what Vine thinks by scanning his facial features is unsuccessful. He, too, is unknowable.

During the pilgrimage, Clarel finds Rolfe's viewpoint more amenable than Vine's. Rolfe is an adventurer who closely resembles Melville himself. He has traveled widely, but he has also read widely. His personality has been shaped by both activities. "Though given to study," Rolfe "supplemented Plato's theme / With daedal life in boats and tents / A messmate of the elements" (*W*, XII, p. 96). Clarel never settles on any one outlook and never really resolves his religious doubts, but he draws increasingly close to Rolfe's way of thinking as the poem progresses.

Clarel's characteristic behavior shows during the approach to the mountains of Moab. While Rolfe and Derwent enjoy an animated conversation as the pilgrims near Mt Pisgah, Clarel attentively listens to what they are saying. The narrator explains, "Clarel, receptive, saw and heard, / Learning, unlearning, word by word." Clarel's personal and intellectual growth not only involves new information and ideas, it also requires him to rethink what he knows and discard previous ideas when they no longer apply, an aspect of his character Melville had emphasized since the beginning of the poem. In the first canto, Clarel says to himself that only by "unlearning" will he be able to open "the expanse of time's vast sea" (*W*, XII, pp. 177, 5). The quest offered a traditional pattern for the epic hero. Melville made the pursuit of knowledge Clarel's heroic quest.

An epic community, that is, a coherent group of people sharing the same nationality or religion or set of values is another essential component of the epic. In Berryman's *Dream Songs*, America functions as the epic community. In *Clarel*, the band of pilgrims forms the immediate community. Together they constitute a microcosm of a much broader community, the Judeo-Christian world. From a literary point of view, the travel narrative provides the link between microcosm and macrocosm. In the nineteenth century, tales of travel to the Holy Land formed a significant subgenre of English and American travel literature. Think of *The Innocents Aboard*, Mark Twain's uproarious narrative of his trip to Europe and the Holy Land. Books of travel let fireside people participate vicariously in the journey to the Holy Land. Most travel writers let their readers appreciate the Holy Land from the perspective of a devout Christian. Mark Twain portrayed the Holy Land from a satirical point of view. *Clarel* embodies Melville's skepticism.

Paradoxically, the pilgrims in *Clarel* share communal aspects that contradict the idea of community. Agath fled his home in Egypt to escape the plague and ended up the sole survivor of a shipwreck. Djalea, though the son of an emir, has been exiled from his home. Mortmain, having exiled himself from Europe, now wanders the world. Rolfe has been a rover in the South Seas. Ungar, formerly a Confederate officer, exiled himself from the United States after the Civil War and now works as a mercenary in the Near East. Exiles, loners, rovers, wanderers: the pilgrims in *Clarel* form a community of men who have deserted the original communities to which they belonged.

Commenting on the alienation so many of the pilgrims in *Clarel* share, Bezanson identified a sense of loss as another communal aspect the characters share. Nearly all have experienced loss in their lives. Clarel has not, however, at least not until he returns to Jerusalem to find Ruth dead. As Bezanson observed, the poem's love plot gives Clarel a sense of loss and thus lets him join the community of others who have experienced loss (*W*, XII, pp. 578–579).

The community Melville imagined for his epic is actually more modern than the epic communities that occur later in modern American verse. Later epics such as Ezra Pound's *Cantos* and William Carlos Williams's *Paterson* establish communities that unify the work and provide a shared set of values. Melville's epic community is an anti-community, one whose defining characteristics are negative ones. Absence, alienation, exile, loss: these are the attributes that define the epic community in *Clarel*.

Epic dignity is largely a function of poetics. There is no pre-established rhythmic, metrical, stanzaic, or generic pattern the epic must follow. It should be a poem, of course, but some even lift this requirement. *Moby-Dick*, for example, has often been called an epic. Padraic Colum found that in terms of its theme and its rhythmic prose style *Moby-Dick* had a greater affinity to the epic than the novel.[47] Regardless, a poem must possess a certain dignity to qualify as an epic.

In his preface to *Paradise Lost*, Milton argued against the use of rhyme, which he thought detracted from the dignity of an epic by giving verse a jingling sound. Furthermore, rhyme restricts the poet's expression whereas blank verse offers greater freedom of expression. Melville's decision to write *Clarel* in rhymed tetrameter verse, while indebted to the narrative poems of Sir Walter Scott, challenges the ideas Milton expressed. But perhaps Milton and Melville did not disagree as much as the differences between their poetics suggest. Milton eschewed rhyme because he found it confining; Melville chose rhyme because he found it confining. The author of the long, flowing sentences of *Moby-Dick* intentionally forced himself to write in the cramped space of irregularly rhymed tetrameter verse when he came to *Clarel*.

While appreciating selected passages, contemporary reviewers found the quality of verse in *Clarel* uneven. Throughout *Clarel*, eloquent lines are interspersed with harsh, awkward passages. One reviewer observed, "There are fragments of fresh, musical lyrics, suggestive both of Hafiz and of William Blake; there are passages so rough, distorted, and commonplace withal, that the reader impatiently shuts the book." The reviewer for *The Academy* shrewdly recognized that the harshness of Melville's verse was intentional: "The form is subordinate to the matter, and a rugged inattention to niceties of rhyme and meter here and there seems rather deliberate than careless" (*CR*, pp. 532, 538). An irregular world deserves irregular verse.

The form of *Clarel* parallels its content. Its juxtaposition of lyric and discordant passages reflects its juxtaposition of seemingly contradictory ideas. Continuing his appreciation, the reviewer for *The Academy* noticed Melville's "subtle blending of old and new thought," "unexpected turns of argument," and "the hidden connexion between things outwardly separate." Juxtaposing distant objects to reveal heretofore unrecognized connections, Melville exemplified an aesthetic that would not emerge until the twentieth century. The method he used in *Clarel* anticipates an approach Pierre Reverdy defined four decades later: "The image is a pure creation of the mind. It cannot be born from a comparison but from a juxtaposition of two more or less distant realities. The more the relationship between the two juxtaposed realities is distant and true, the stronger the image will be – the greater its emotional power and poetic reality."[48]

Alluding to "Hugh of Lincoln" in Part 4, Melville juxtaposed distant-but-true objects to create a powerful image. Based on an old legend, "Hugh of Lincoln" is a traditional ballad with a long-standing reputation: Chaucer retold the legend in "The Prioress's Tale." While playing ball, Hugh of Lincoln accidentally kicks his ball through the window of a Jew's house. The Jew's daughter catches the boy. As punishment, she gruesomely slaughters him.[49] Melville turned this traditional story into an analogue for child abuse in modern-day factories. Ungar queries: "How many Hughs of Lincoln, say, / Does Mammon in his mills, to-day, / Crook, if he do not crucify?" (*W*, XII, p. 414). Suddenly, the intervening centuries collapse, and the reader recognizes the aptness of Melville's parallel. The violence of this centuries-old story, multiplied by many thousand, becomes real on the shop floor of the modern factory. Melville's use of this traditional ballad contributes to the epic dignity of *Clarel*, even as it captures the indignities of modern existence.

Offering some general thoughts on the epic in the conclusion to his study, Patrick White observed, "An epic is a life's work. Depicting the whole of life of a community and defining its essence at the same time are not easy tasks. Fighting the battle to find the new and better mode of expression to carry it through the length and depth demanded by the epic takes the most sharply-honed and disciplined poetic mind and craft."[50] Melville's experience bears out White's observation.

Clarel was not exactly a life's work, but it did take Melville two decades to complete it, counting from the time of his journey to the Holy Land in 1856 to the book's publication in 1876. The poem could be backdated even further. *Clarel* contains numerous personal references that recall episodes from Melville's early life and passages from his earlier books. The image of the stormy petrel, a sea bird imbued with a rich tradition of sailor superstitions, let him create an epic simile that echoes both *Moby-Dick* and "The Encantadas."[51] Considering the amount of personal experience that went into the poem, one can consider *Clarel* a life's work.

As it neared completion, *Clarel* seemed to take over Melville's life. His family thought so. Many years later, his daughter Frances recalled being "roused from sleep at two in the morning to read proof with her father of a long, obscure poem on the Holy Land" (*W*, XII, p. 659). Writing to a sympathetic correspondent while *Clarel* was in press, Elizabeth Melville described her husband's mood: "Herman, poor fellow, is in such a frightfully nervous state, and particularly now with such an added strain on his mind, that I am actually *afraid* to have any one here for fear that he will be upset entirely, and not be able to go on with the printing . . . If ever this dreadful *incubus* of a *book* (I call it so because it has undermined all our happiness) gets off Herman's shoulders I do hope he may be in better mental health" (*W*, XII, p. 539).

Writing often led Melville to the brink of psychic exhaustion. He described the process in "House of the tragic poet": "Without the *afflatus* it is in vain to undertake poetry. The afflatus is simply intoxication, more or less. The poem completed, the debauch comes to an end; and the bard's Blue Monday begins. The nerves of the poet are in a shattered condition."[52] As Melville brought *Clarel* to an end, he still had not resolved the problems Clarel faced at the poem's beginning. Clarel continues to doubt his faith; he still questions the relevance of faith in the modern world. Of course, Clarel's experience is not unique. The clash between faith and science is central to much Victorian poetry. There may be better poems that treat this topic, but there are none that imbue it with epic grandeur more than *Clarel*.

The return to prose: Burgundy Club sketches, *John Marr*

In addition to *Battle-Pieces* and *Clarel*, Melville wrote much other poetry during the last three decades of his life. By the mid-1870s, he had drafted two fairly long poems, which he would ultimately call "At the Hostelry" and "Naples in the Time of Bomba." Both show the influence Robert Browning's work was having on Melville. John Freeman called these two poems "curiously Browning-like exercises, simpler than Browning in phrase, but no less picturesque and careless in movement."[53] In light of his commitment to poetry, Melville's disavowal of prose fiction seemed complete by the time he finished *Clarel*. But after seeing

Clarel through the press, he returned to these Browning-like exercises and did something very un-Browning-like. One of the great joys (and great challenges) of reading a Browning poem is discerning the persona and predicament of its speaker as the verse monologue unfolds. Giving his readers no advance notice, Browning put the burden of interpretation on them. Melville, alternatively, drafted prose headnotes introducing these two poems to help readers understand them.

Paradise Lost, each book of which is prefaced by a prose "argument" describing what it is about, generally inspired Melville's headnotes. A reviewer's comment may have supplied the immediate inspiration: "The thread of the story which *Clarel* contains the reader will find some difficulty in deciphering. If Mr. Melville had condescended to follow the example of Milton, he might have eased the reader's task by placing before his poem an 'argument'" (*CR*, p. 536). As he composed them, Melville's headnotes became much more than Milton's arguments. In Melville's hands they turned into delightful little vignettes that brought alive the world of a fictional gentleman's club he called the Burgundy Club. Melville obviously enjoyed imagining this club and its members. Unable to stop with the two headnotes, he wrote some supplementary sketches, too. Though he set aside the Burgundy Club sketches in the 1870s, he returned to them in the mid-1880s, when he started assembling them as a complete book. He even drafted a charming introduction entitled, "House of the tragic poet," which forms a self-reflexive comment on the publication process.

The Burgundy Club sounds like a wonderful place. Here, younger members of the club could listen to their elders tell stories of personal adventure from times past in a convivial atmosphere. Major John Gentian, a Civil War hero who had lost an arm in combat, best represents the club as a whole. The narrator of a sketch entitled, "To Major John Gentian, Dean of the Burgundy Club," characterizes the genial nature of the major's "club-chat." Gentian garnishes his talk with "sprigs of classic parsley set about it or inserted cloves of old English proverbs, or yet older Latin ones equally commonplace, yet never losing the verity in them, their preservative spice" (*Works*, XIII, p. 358).

If proverbs provide the spice, the meat of the major's discourse is the personal narrative. The narrator of "To Major John Gentian" explains, "Pleasant it is when weary of the never-ending daily news, the same sort of thing forever, how pleasant to be spirited back by a tale, by some veteran's living voice and eloquent gestures, to a period that is no news at all." Throughout his life, Melville had enjoyed listening to the tales older men told. The listening experience he attributes to White Jacket encapsulates his own. White Jacket "always endeavored to draw out the oldest Tritons into narratives of the war-service they had seen. There were but few of them, it is true, who had been in action;

but that only made their narratives the more valuable" (*Works*, XIII, p. 366; *W*, V, p. 311).

For Melville, oral history had a unique quality that lifted it above written history, as his portrayal of Jack Gentian suggests. His emphasis on Gentian's voice and gestures imply that there are elements of storytelling that extend beyond the verbal text. Furthermore, the narrator of "To Major John Gentian" expresses great satisfaction that the major's personal Civil War stories will not be "formalised into professed history" (*Works*, XIII, p. 365). The narrator's attitude toward written history parallels Melville's refusal to let Nathaniel Hawthorne review *Moby-Dick*. Melville wanted Hawthorne's appreciation to remain private, to be something between the two of them. Told within the confines of a private club, Gentian's war stories are narratives shared solely between teller and listener. Unlike written works, they are subjected to neither the scrutiny of the narrow-minded critic nor the judgement of the fickle public, which Melville compared to "an unknown island at the ends of the earth" in "House of the tragic poet."[54] These personal narratives belong to Gentian and the few sensitive club members he chooses to tell.

The story of Melville's life contains numerous incidents of stories told by old timers. While in England in 1849, he visited Greenwich Hospital, where he met pensioners from the Royal Navy, at least one of whom had served with Lord Nelson at Trafalgar. Melville briefly recorded the experience in his journal, a work whose literary qualities differ significantly from his published works. In place of the long, flowing sentences that fill his novels, the journal entries typically take the form of short sentence fragments possessing a poignant, piercing, staccato quality. On this occasion he wrote, "Walked in Greenwich Park. Observatory. Fine view from a hill – talk with an old pensioner there." He remembered this experience and elaborated upon it in *Billy Budd*. Discussing some naval irregularities, the narrator of *Billy Budd* remembers the information being "personally communicated to me now more than forty years ago by an old pensioner in a cocked hat with whom I had a most interesting talk on the terrace at Greenwich, a Baltimore Negro, a Trafalgar man" (*W*, XV, p. 23; *BB*, p. 66).

Recalling this forty-year-old encounter during the composition of *Billy Budd*, Melville not only remembered the man he met at Greenwich, he also remembered the story that man told. Since this encounter, the older man's memories fused with Melville's own. Piggybacking the reminiscences of others onto his own memory, Melville formed links that personally connected him to history and extended his backward glance to the eighteenth century.

Though Melville imagined the gentleman's club as an ideal place where conversation could bring the past alive, he avoided joining any of the prominent clubs of his day. Reading Melville's charming descriptions of the Burgundy Club, one cannot help but wonder why he did not join any of the New York clubs. Given his travel experiences, his fondness for cozy interior spaces, his enjoyment of Scottish ale and good cigars, and his penchant for good conversation, Melville had the makings of an ideal club member. Prominent clubmen who knew him greatly enjoyed his company. Richard Lathers, an active member of the Lotos Club in New York, had a summer house in Pittsfield and often visited Melville at Arrowhead, where he "listened with intense pleasure to his highly individual views of society and politics. He always supplied a bountiful supply of good cider – the product of his own orchard – and of tobacco, in the virtues of which he was a firm believer" (*Log*, I, p. 479). Lathers almost surely invited him to join the Lotos Club, but Melville declined. William Cramer, to take another friend for example, also recorded Melville's predilection for clubs and club life. Attending a lecture Melville presented in Milwaukee, Cramer found it quite different from the typical public lecture. It was more like "a feast as one would like to sit down to in a club room . . . with the blue smoke of a meerschaum gracefully curling and floating away" (*W*, IX, p. 526).

Others tried to coax him to join their clubs. Bayard Taylor, a prominent travel writer Melville had met many years earlier, invited him to join the Travelers Club in the 1860s. The offer sounded tempting. Taylor explained that regular members included Albert Bierstadt, whose landscapes possess a sense of grandeur not dissimilar to Melville's greatest writings, and Townsend Harris, who, as consul to Japan, had negotiated the earliest United States treaties with that nation. There is no indication that Melville accepted Taylor's invitation. Once the Travelers Club was formally organized, he was made an honorary member.[55] He never became an active member.

The Authors Club, "composed of gentlemen devoted to a distinctively literary life" who came together in the 1880s, invited Melville to join. Knowing his reputation for reclusiveness, Charles De Kay, one of the founding members, was somewhat surprised when Melville accepted an invitation to the club's organizational meeting. The *New York Times* (24 November 1882) listed Melville's name among "gentlemen present, or who expressed by letter or by proxy an interest in the movement." Though Melville initially expressed interest in the club, he never showed. After sending De Kay his acceptance, he wrote a follow-up letter, explaining that he "had become too much of a hermit," asserting that he could no longer stand large gatherings," and withdrawing his acceptance. Not only did he refuse invitations to join the prominent clubs of the day, he also refused dinner invitations. When Abraham Lansing invited him to the Fort Orange Club in Albany, Melville turned down the invitation, calling himself an old fogey (*Log*, II, p. 781; *W*, XIV, p. 475).

The fictional Burgundy Club offered him a distinct advantage over real clubs. With the Burgundy Club, Melville could imagine conviviality while preserving his solitude, an impulse that was becoming increasingly precious to him. Despite his ability to write very quickly, Melville had realized that time and solitude were the surest ways for him to cultivate his literary abilities. In his copy of Isaac Disraeli's *The Literary Character; or The History of Men of Genius*, he scored a passage discussing how important time and solitude were to authors:

> If there were not periods when they shall allow their days to melt harmoniously into each other, if they do not pass whole weeks together in their study, without intervening absences, they will not be admitted into the last recess of the Muses. Whether their glory come from researches, or from enthusiasm, time, with not a feather ruffled on his wings, time alone opens discoveries and kindles meditation. This desert of solitude, so vast and so dreary to the man of the world, to the man of genius is the magical garden of Armida, whose enchantments arose amidst solitude, while solitude was everywhere among those enchantments.[56]

Retiring from his post as customs inspector at the end of 1885, Melville finally had the time and solitude he had sought for so long. He was loathe to relinquish them.

If the Authors Club could have provided the kind of conversation Melville attributed to Jack Gentian, perhaps he might have joined. Sixty-six at the time of his retirement, however, he saw little opportunity to hear the kind of stories he liked best within the Authors Club. Most of its founding members were younger men. Melville would be one of the club's old timers. As a club member, he would be forced into the role of teller, not listener. He would be the one younger members sought out for stories of times past. In other words, he would continually be called upon to retell the story of *Typee*, a story he had long since grown weary of retelling.

In a way, Melville had become the man he imagined as the narrator of "I and My Chimney," who explains, "Old myself, I take to oldness in things; for that cause mainly loving old Montaigne, and old cheese, and old wine; and eschewing young people, hot rolls, new books, and early potatoes" (*W*, IX, p. 361). Avoiding the Authors Club, Melville was eschewing young people. He was also preventing himself from having to recall his romantic past on demand. Melville's personal memories were quite special to him. He enjoyed recalling them but did not always want to share them.

The importance of memory to Melville is obvious from other poems he was composing late in life. "John Marr," the lead poem of *John Marr and Other*

Sailors with some Sea-Pieces, the collection of verse he had privately printed in 1888, reflects Melville's mental state during the last years of his life. He also wrote a headnote for "John Marr," which recounts the story of Marr's life and fills in the background to the poem. A career sailor whose debilitating injury prevents him from returning to sea, Marr ventures inland, where he establishes a small farm and marries – only to watch his young wife and infant child perish. He buries them and vows to spend the rest of his days near their burial place. His personal past as a sailor alienates him from his farmer-neighbors, whose inland experience prevents them from relating to what he has to say. Unable to develop new friendships, Marr seeks company and solace in his memories.

All this background detail occurs in the lengthy headnote to "John Marr," which overshadows the poem it is intended to introduce. Not only is the headnote much longer than the poem, it possesses a haunting quality the poem itself lacks. Given its melancholy tone and poetic diction, this headnote comes closer to an Ossianic prose poem than a Miltonic argument. Late in life, Melville's genius was pulling him back to prose.

The books he was reading the last years of his life confirm his renewed interest in fiction. On 31 May 1890, he withdrew from the New York Society Library *A Hazard of New Fortunes*, a novel by one of the foremost practitioners of literary realism, William Dean Howells. This urban novel culminates in violence arising from the labor unrest associated with a strike by streetcar employees. Two weeks later, Melville returned Howells to the library. Instead of borrowing any more works by him or any of the other realists, Melville withdrew two old favorites by Sir Walter Scott, *Peveril of the Peak*, a historical romance centered around Titus Oates's Popish Plot, and *Quentin Durward*, the story of a young Scottish mercenary set in fifteenth-century France (*Log*, II, p. 825). In other words, after gratifying his curiosity about realist writing, Melville returned to historical romance, stories of the past told through the haze of time and imagination.

Melville never did finish assembling all his Burgundy Club material together as a book. His rediscovery of prose fiction helps explain why. So do the comments on time and solitude Melville marked in his copy of Disraeli. Drafting the Burgundy Club sketches, the headnote to "John Marr," and a handful of miscellaneous sketches including "Daniel Orme," a sailor's character sketch, Melville recaptured his passion for prose. Time and solitude let him unravel the problems he was having with the Burgundy Club sketches and allowed him to understand how to reshape his materials.

One passage in "The Marquis de Grandvin," another of the Burgundy Club sketches, contains the kernel of an idea Melville would develop at length. Describing clubmen in general, the narrator observes, "They have a suggestion of the potentialities in the unvitiated Adam, a creature, according to hallowed authority, originally created but a little lower than the angels. Almost invariably these men have physical beauty; and the moral charm is in keeping with that, apparently a spontaneous emanation from it" (*Works*, XIII, p. 349). Time and solitude let Melville know that a contemporary New York club was not the best place to locate this new Adam. A better place to put him would be the forecastle of a man-of-war from the previous century. Time and solitude let Melville transform his ideal clubman into a handsome sailor named Billy Budd.

Billy Budd: visions and revisions

The last part of *Billy Budd, Sailor* – a poem written in the form of a Browning-like dramatic monologue entitled "Billy in the Darbies" – is the first part Melville wrote. Having drafted the poem, he composed a brief headnote to put it in context. Structurally, the early headnote-and-poem version of *Billy Budd* resembles "John Marr." Melville may have planned to include "Billy in the Darbies" as part of *John Marr and Other Sailors*, but he gradually made other plans for the story of Billy Budd. Recognizing its inherent potential, he revised and greatly expanded the work. His editors have identified numerous stages and substages of composition. For simplicity's sake, three basic phases can be delineated: the early headnote-and-poem, a middle version about the size of a longish short story, and a near-final, book-length version (*BB*, p. 2). To appreciate *Billy Budd*, it is essential to understand the compositional process the work underwent. As he developed his characters, Melville found a way to dramatize what he was thinking about in terms of good and evil, nature and civilization.

The earliest surviving leaves of the *Billy Budd* manuscript date from 1886; Melville may have begun the work as early as the year before (*BB*, p. 274). Though a product of his final lustrum, *Billy Budd* contains ideas he had been brooding over since his sailor days. The personal experiences the narrator recalls closely parallel Melville's own. Furthermore, the story's general theme reflects ideas he had articulated in previous writings.

A piece he wrote in 1849 provides a key to understanding how he initially conceived the character of Billy Budd. In a review entitled "Mr. Parkman's Tour," he commented on the disdainful attitude toward native people that occasionally shows through Francis Parkman's *California and Oregon Trail*. Refuting Parkman, Melville minimized cultural differences and stressed the fundamental equality of all men: "We are all of us – Anglo-Saxons, Dyaks and Indians – sprung from one head and made in one image. . . . And wherever we recognize the image of God let us reverence it; though it swing from the gallows" (*W*, IX, pp. 231–232). Melville's words offer a different take on the Christian concept of the "human face divine." Though he had used this idea sardonically in his first book, his reuse of it in "Mr. Parkman's Tour" has a respectful tone – despite its inherent irony.

Moby-Dick provides Melville's fullest articulation of the idea of the human face divine:

> Man, in the ideal, is so noble and so sparkling, such a grand and glowing creature, that over any ignominious blemish in him all his fellows should run to throw their costliest robes. That immaculate manliness we feel within ourselves, so far within us, that it remains intact though all the outer character seem gone; bleeds with keenest anguish at the undraped spectacle of a valor-ruined man. Nor can piety itself, at such a shameful sight, completely stifle her upbraidings against the permitting stars. But this august dignity I treat of, is not the dignity of kings and robes, but that abounding dignity which has no robed investiture. Thou shalt see it shining in the arm that wields a pick or drives a spike; that democratic dignity which, on all hands, radiates without end from God; Himself! The great God absolute! The centre and circumference of all democracy! His omnipresence, our divine equality!   (*W*, VI, p. 117)

Even Ahab manifests the idea of man's godliness. Captain Peleg calls him "a grand, ungodly, god-like man" (*W*, VI, p. 79). The epithet may seem oxymoronic, but from Melville's perspective, a man could very well be both ungodly and god-like. Those who attempt to defy the gods may be heading toward annihilation, but they do not, they cannot diminish their own god-like nature. The person with the blackest soul on earth still possesses a human face divine.

Though derived from a religious notion, Melville's concept of man's godlike dignity is essentially secular, as some of his other writings suggest. In a letter to Hawthorne, he provided a democratic reformulation of the idea: "A thief in jail is as honorable a personage as Gen. George Washington" (*W*, XIV, pp. 190–191). Equating a thief with Washington or, for that matter, equating Queequeg and Washington, Melville shifted focus from the god-like nature of all men to the essential humanity of all men. Even the criminal convicted of a capital crime deserves to be treated humanely.

In the headnote-and-poem version of *Billy Budd*, Melville's title character *is* a criminal. No doubt about it: Billy is guilty of leading a mutiny. An early draft of the poem presents his thoughts prior to his execution and reveals Billy's culpability. "Our little game's up," he says. The sole surviving manuscript leaf of the early headnote supplies further information about how Melville initially saw his hero. It identifies Billy not as the foretopman he would become in the second phase of the story but as the captain of a gun's crew aboard a man-of-war, a rank more appropriate for an older sailor. The manuscript headnote also explains that Billy was "summarily condemned at sea to be hung as the ring leader of an incipient mutiny" (*BB*, pp. 277, 275).

Regardless of Billy's culpability or his maturity, Melville's earliest concept of him does share one essential aspect with the young and innocent sailor he would become in Melville's final concept. Early and late, Billy is the stereotypical handsome sailor. As the manuscript headnote indicates, he is "not only genial in temper, and sparklingly so, but in person also goodly to behold" (*BB*, p. 275). In short, the early version of *Billy Budd* provides a specific example of the general image Melville described in "Mr. Parkman's Tour": the face divine swinging from the gallows pole.

While writing *Billy Budd*, Melville encountered similar manifestations of this idea that reinforced what he was thinking. Reading Balzac's *Séraphita*, for example, he check-marked and partially underlined the following question: "How came it that Evil, king of the earth, was born of a God supremely good in His essence and in His faculties, who can produce nothing that is not made in His own image?" Not only did Balzac articulate the idea of evil men made in God's image, he also offered imagery anticipating Billy's execution in the final version of *Billy Budd*. Later in *Séraphita*, Melville scored the following passage: "How many a pardoned Angel has passed from martyrdom to heaven! Sinai, Golgotha are not in this place nor in that; Angels are crucified in every place, in every sphere." The Balzac revival in America coincided with Melville's composition of *Billy Budd*. Melville got caught up in it, read numerous Balzac works, and recognized in him a kindred spirit. *Séraphita* anticipates ideas Melville would develop in *Billy Budd*.[57]

As he revised the work, Melville expanded the prose headnote to the length of a Henry James short story. The most significant addition he made during this second phase of composition involves John Claggart, who was emerging as a major character. To get from the earliest known version of *Billy Budd* to the middle version in which Claggart figures prominently, Melville essentially bifurcated his initial concept of Billy. Claggart possesses many characteristics similar to the early Billy. Melville initially made Claggart forty years old, an age that roughly corresponds to Billy's age in the early concept of him. He also gave Claggart a high-ranking position of master-at-arms, much as he had made Billy the captain of a gun's crew. And he made Claggart handsome, giving him facial features "cleanly cut as those on a Greek medallion" (*BB*, p. 316). Claggart's handsomeness differs greatly from Billy's. Whereas Billy possesses the rugged good looks of a man who lives and works outdoors the year round, Claggart has the pale, delicate features of a chartered accountant who has spent his life before a ledger.

Claggart's handsomeness reflects Melville's ongoing interest in physiognomy. "Daniel Orme" contains what may be Melville's last word on the subject. Discussing its relationship to art and using Titian and Gilbert Stuart as examples, he observed, "A profound portrait-painter like Titian or our famous countryman Stewart, what such an observer sees in any face he may earnestly study, that essentially is the man. To disentangle his true history from contemporary report is superfluous. Not so with us who are scarce Titians and Stewarts" (*Works*, XIII, p. 117). In other words, great artists possess a special combination of intuition, genius, and perception allowing them to discern the inner self by reading a person's face. Those of us who lack the qualities of a great artist cannot. Claggart's physical appearance reflects the difficulties involved with interpreting a man's character based solely on his appearance.

"Daniel Orme" parallels *Billy Budd* not only for what it says about physiognomy but also for the characteristics its title character shares with John Claggart. Of Orme's early history "it may verily be said that nobody knew anything but himself." Similarly, nothing is known of Claggart's early life. To describe both characters, Melville drew figures of speech from metallurgy and metalwork, but his similes reveal the differences between the characters. Whereas Claggart's features are cut like a medallion, Orme's are "cast as in iron." Furthermore, Orme's appearance is marred by marks from an explosive charge that peppered his face "all below the eyes with dense dottings of black-blue" (*Works*, XIII, p. 118). The difference between the physical appearance of these two characters determines how their fellow sailors react to them. Orme's mysterious background and menacing appearance allows his fellow crew members to read all sorts of evil in his face – regardless that the marks left by the explosion were purely a matter of chance. Claggart's handsomeness masks his evil.

Deriving Claggart's character partly from his initial concept of Billy, Melville had to go back and revise Billy's in order to differentiate the two as much as possible. In revision, Melville demoted Billy from captain of a gun's crew to foretopman and made him much younger. In the final version, Billy is twenty-one years old. Most importantly, Melville removed Billy's propensity for malice. No longer is he capable of fomenting mutiny. Now, he is merely the object of Claggart's malicious accusations. Both are products of nature, but Claggart represents natural evil whereas Billy symbolizes natural goodness. Melville's language reinforces their opposition. Having compared Claggart's appearance to the face on a medallion, he reused the image of a coin, calling Claggart a "peculiar human creature the direct reverse of a saint" (*BB*, p. 331). Claggart and Billy are two sides of the same coin.

Though Melville lengthened his story in this second phase of composition, he actually simplified it. In the headnote-and-poem version, Billy's character – good-natured yet capable of malice – is more complex. The second phase presents a fairly straightforward binary opposition: good versus evil – "the clash of absolutes" John Middleton Murry called it (*CR*, p. 550). Recognizing the oversimplification, Melville made further revisions as he delineated the nature of Claggart's evil tendencies.

In a preliminary description of Claggart's character, Melville had given him "an evil nature, not engendered by vicious training or corrupting books or licentious living, but self-subsisting and innate, in short 'a depravity according to nature.'" Revising this passage, he made two key changes. In the revised version, Claggart has "the mania of an evil nature, not engendered by vicious training or corrupting books or licentious living, but born with him and innate, in short 'a depravity according to nature'" (*BB*, pp. 336, 76).

The revision makes ambiguous the precise status of Claggart's evil. Adding the words "the mania of" Melville altered Claggart's evil nature from something immutable and unchanging to a mental affliction that could ebb and flow according to circumstance. Claggart remains inherently evil from one version of *Billy Budd* to the next, but Melville's revision lets his evil vary by degrees. Deleting the adjective "self-subsisting" – a favorite phrase of Kant and Coleridge – in favor of "born with him," Melville reinforced the changeable nature of Claggart's evil.

A. R. Humphreys has called Melville's analysis of Claggart's character one of the finest things in all of Melville's work: "The analysis is probing, adumbrative, quietly troubled, and more interesting than any sensationalism could be. It presents, one might say, original sin according to agnosticism."[58] Once he had developed Claggart's character and elaborated Billy's to enhance the contrast between the two, Melville assumed he was close to finishing *Billy Budd* and began making a fair copy of the manuscript. As he recopied the work, he reconceived it yet again. Melville recognized how to enhance the complexity of his story in a bold and challenging new way: he would give Captain Vere a major role in the unfolding drama. To understand the part Vere plays, it is essential to realize that Melville worked out Claggart's character before he developed Vere's, an aspect of *Billy Budd* that is obscured by the fact that important passages describing Vere's personality occur in the final version of the story prior to passages describing Claggart's personality.[59]

Captain Vere bears little resemblance to the sea captains in Melville's previous works.[60] Unlike the others, Vere was not inspired by captains Melville had known; he was created to suit the story of Billy Budd as it was developing. In a way, Vere grew out of Claggart. Much as Melville had formed Claggart partly by dividing his initial concept of Billy in two, he formed Vere by borrowing attributes from Claggart. Describing Captain Vere, Melville made him about forty years old – the same age as Claggart. Subsequently realizing that he had made them both the same age, Melville went back through the manuscript and changed Claggart's age to thirty-five.

Claggart and Vere share other attributes. The two are well read, and they have similar tastes and similar manners. Like Claggart, Vere also seems ill at ease aboard a man-of-war. Both share a similar level of education. Claggart's "general aspect and manner were so suggestive of an education and career incongruous with his naval function that when not actively engaged in it he looked like a man of high quality, social and moral, who for reasons of his own was keeping incog." Similarly, Vere's long naval service "had not resulted in absorbing and *salting* the entire man. He had a marked leaning toward everything intellectual. He loved books, never going to sea without a newly replenished library, compact but of the best" (*BB*, pp. 64, 62). The similarities between the two characters stem from the fact that Melville never completely finished revising *Billy Budd* once he reconceived the work. Borrowing characteristics from Claggart to develop Captain Vere, he never went back through his manuscript to distinguish the two characters fully.

Vere's presence greatly enhances the story's complexity. In its second phase, *Billy Budd* had become a tale of good versus evil. The inclusion of Captain Vere as a major character adds another dimension to the story. A man-of-war, as *White-Jacket* had so eloquently demonstrated, is both an icon and microcosm of the civilization it defends. As the captain of a man-of-war, Vere represents that civilization. As exemplars of good and evil, Billy and Claggart represent nature. In other words, the third phase of *Billy Budd* introduces a second opposition to the story: nature versus civilization.

The clash between nature and civilization that emerges in this phase of composition does not supplant the clash between good and evil that had controlled the second phase of the story. *Billy Budd* achieves its complexity as these two sets of opposing pairs compete to control the narrative. Whereas the opposition between good and evil is a clash of absolutes, the opposition between nature and civilization is not, as Claggart's behavior demonstrates. While he and Billy represent nature, Claggart, unlike Billy, can use civilization to his advantage.[61] Discussing the presence of "natural depravity" among men, Melville observed, "Civilization, especially if of the austerer sort, is auspicious to it. It folds itself in the mantle of respectability" (*BB*, p. 75). Like the Confidence Man, Claggart blends into his surroundings and insinuates his evil among the oblivious denizens of the civilized world.

Once Claggart has accused Billy of mutiny, Captain Vere summons both men to his stateroom so that Billy may face his accuser. Hearing the accusation,

Billy's natural defect – a stress-induced stutter – prevents him from speaking. He responds the only way he can, instinctually: he punches his accuser in the face. The blow knocks Claggart dead. While Vere recognizes that Billy did not kill Claggart intentionally, he refuses to consider any other option beyond the one dictated by his interpretation of maritime law. Once this tragic event occurs, Vere quickly decides what to do. To the ship's surgeon, who has pronounced Claggart dead, Vere exclaims, "Struck dead by an angel of God! Yet the angel must hang!" (*BB*, p. 101).

In the second phase of *Billy Budd*, only a few leaves separate the killing of Claggart and the poem that ends the work. In the third major phase of composition, Melville greatly elaborated the story of Billy's trial (*BB*, p. 2). Vere's actions after Claggart's death seem designed to assure Billy's execution. Instead of putting Billy in the brig and waiting to consult his superiors, he calls an immediate drumhead court. (The term comes from the battlefield, where courts martial used an upturned drum in lieu of a judge's bench.) At Billy's trial, Captain Vere delivers a speech assuring that the officers he has placed on the court will convict Billy of a capital crime.

The late revisions not only develop Captain Vere's character, they also heighten the story's ambiguity. Melville deliberately altered passages to avoid telling the reader how to interpret the captain's decisions.[62] Should Vere have proceeded with the drumhead court as an attempt to assert his authority and forestall other potential mutinies? Or should he have waited to try Billy after consulting with his superiors? While eliciting such questions in his reader's mind, Melville left them unanswered. Readers must decide for themselves the rightness of Vere's actions.

The character of Billy Budd is often considered a Christ figure. Melville made the link between the two explicit as he compared a chip off the yardarm from which Billy is hanged to a piece of the true cross. But the comparison is imprecise. Christ died for man's sins. Billy dies for the sake of civilization. The poem that closes the final version of *Billy Budd* reiterates the image of Billy's execution and thus brings together the opposition between nature and civilization. Sanctioned by statute and handed down by a court of law, the sentence of capital punishment is the civilized equivalent of a primitive ritual sacrifice. In the act of capital punishment, nature and civilization coincide. The opposition between good and evil is irrelevant in the end. The execution of Billy – natural man – is the blood sacrifice essential for civilization to survive.

Chapter 4

Reception

"A howling cheese": so Robert Louis Stevenson described Herman Melville in an 1888 letter written aboard a schooner bound for the South Seas. Stevenson's unusual epithet may seem derogatory but his figurative expression is actually quite flattering. It means something similar to the proverbial phrase, "to take the cake." When it came to authors who wrote about the South Seas, Stevenson was saying, Melville took the cake. He was first rate, the real thing, tops – in short – a howling cheese. Elsewhere, Stevenson was less cryptic in his praise of Melville. In one magazine article, he asserted that there are "but two writers who have touched the South Seas with any genius, both Americans: Melville and Charles Warren Stoddard." Overrating Stoddard, Stevenson was paying debt to an important influence. When the two had met in San Francisco earlier, Stoddard presented him with copies of *Typee* and *Omoo*, which Stevenson took with him to the South Seas. Recalling their fond conversations, Stevenson observed, "It was in such talks, which we were both eager to repeat, that I first heard the names – first fell under the spell – of the islands; and it was from one of the first of them that I returned (a happy man) with *Omoo* under one arm, and my friend's own adventures under the other."[1]

Stevenson was a member of a small but slowly expanding group of British litterateurs who were discovering Melville for themselves in the 1880s and giving him the kind of critical attention he had not received since *Typee* and *Omoo* first appeared four decades earlier. In Melville's lifetime, the general trajectory of his critical reception had gone from great enthusiasm to near-total neglect. According to many contemporary readers, Herman Melville – "the author of *Typee*" – never lived up to the potential his first book suggested. Upon its release, *Omoo* confirmed his talent as a highly skilled author of picaresque tales of South Seas adventure, but it never became as popular as *Typee*. There was no Fayaway in *Omoo*.

As his career developed, Melville tried to escape his early reputation as a popular travel writer. Pitching *Mardi* to John Murray, he asked not to be identified as the author of either *Typee* or *Omoo* on the title page of his new book. Murray turned *Mardi* down; his disapproval anticipated the reception it would receive at the hands of contemporary critics. The imaginative and philosophical leaps Melville made in *Mardi* were too much for the readers of adventure travel who so enjoyed *Typee*. A few sensitive souls appreciated *Mardi*, but the general reading public gave it the cold shoulder. After the excesses of *Mardi*, *Redburn* and *White-Jacket* restored Melville's reputation to a certain extent, but never again did he regain the level of fame he had achieved with his first book.

Moby-Dick found some enthusiastic readers when it appeared in 1851, but the book offended many. Americans were disturbed by its seemingly blasphemous passages. Since Richard Bentley had carefully edited passages Christians might find objectionable, British readers found less to complain about on religious grounds but more to complain about on aesthetic ones. The epilogue, where Ishamel explains that he alone survived the wreck of the *Pequod*, was accidentally lost before the book went into production. Bentley put much effort into *The Whale*: it was published as a handsomely-bound triple decker or three-volume set. But no one on Bentley's production staff noticed that the epilogue was missing: *The Whale* was published without it. Reaching the end of the third and final volume, British readers were aghast to discover that they had just read a first-person narrative by a narrator who apparently did not survive.

The daring subject matter of *Pierre* antagonized many who read the book. There were a handful of positive reviews. "One of Melville's rich and entertaining stories," the Albany *Cultivator* called it. "He possesses rare facility in the use of language, and a deep insight into the workings of the mind, when roused by passion, or laboring under extreme excitement."[2] But contemporary readers generally despised the book. This novel about a troubled young man whose incestuous and all-but-explicit love for his sister repulsed readers and irreparably damaged Melville's contemporary reputation.

His short stories were generally well liked, but they did little to further their author's contemporary reputation. Like most contributions to the magazines in his day, Melville's tales appeared anonymously. When he collected several together as *The Piazza Tales*, the book-buying public still found reason to complain. The *Sandusky Commercial Advertiser* (30 June 1856), for example, found *The Piazza Tales* "admirably told and full of a fine vein of humor and romance" but could not help but question the necessity of republishing these previously published works: "It would be much cheaper for the reader to take the magazine and get the literature at first hand and thus save money for books which *are* books, not mere re-publications from the magazines."

Israel Potter received mixed reviews, but even those reviewers who enjoyed the book recognized it as a modest effort far beneath Melville's capacity. Henry Fothergill Chorley asserted that *Israel Potter* did not come close to what William Makepeace Thackery could accomplish in terms of delineating personality. Chorley coined a phrase to characterize Melville's writing style – the earthquake-and-alligator style. Despite the book's faults, he ultimately gave it a positive, if modest recommendation: "not a bad shilling's worth for any railway reader."[3]

The Confidence-Man bewildered all but the most careful readers. George Meredith's review forms one of the best contemporary appreciations. "Few Americans write so powerfully as Mr. Melville, or in better English," Meredith observed. "It required close knowledge of the world, and of the Yankee world, to write such a book and make the satire acute and telling, and the scenes not too improbable for the faith given to fiction. Perhaps the moral is the gullibility of the great Republic, when taken on its own tack."[4] *The Confidence-Man* is often considered vague and obscure, but Meredith's shrewd understanding of the work shows that the best contemporary readers recognized its deeper meanings.

Remaking himself into a poet after the Civil War, Melville failed to revitalize his reputation. *Battle-Pieces*, one of a slew of verse collections published in the war's aftermath, received scant attention in the press. Some readers liked some of the poems. Others disliked the whole collection. One particularly mean-spirited reviewer called *Battle-Pieces* "sad rubbish."[5] The intentionally difficult *Clarel* found few contemporary readers. *Typee* remained in print all the while.

The interest that Stevenson and a handful of others showed in the 1880s continued into the following decade. Henry S. Salt, possibly the greatest Melville aficionado of his generation, observed, "The opinion of those competent judges who are students of Melville's works is so clear and emphatic in his favour, that it is not too much to say that to read his books is generally to appreciate them" (*Doubloon*, p. 113). To support his point, Salt listed several prominent members of England's literary elite, all Melville enthusiasts, including William Morris and W. Clark Russell. Like Salt, Russell did what he could to encourage others to read Melville. He promoted Melville in books, interviews, magazines, and newspapers.

The Boston firm of L. C. Page issued new editions of *Moby-Dick*, *Omoo*, *Typee*, and *White-Jacket* in 1892, the year after Melville's death. Spearheaded by Arthur Stedman, who wrote their biographical and critical introductions, these editions sought to introduce Melville to a new generation of American readers and writers. Samuel Arthur Jones, who first learned about Melville from Henry Salt, acquired all four volumes and read them one after the other. He later compared the experience to what Keats felt upon first looking into Chapman's Homer. Jones said, "I too felt as if a new planet had swam into my ken."[6]

A handful of other readers acquired copies of the Stedman edition. Theodore Dreiser, for one, owned the 1892 edition of *Typee*.[7] For the most part the Stedman edition failed to trigger widespread interest in Melville. In the 1890s, there were no American Salts, no American Russells. The responsibility for promoting Melville in North America fell to a Canadian, Professor Archibald MacMechan of Dalhousie University.

Borrowing an epithet from Russell, MacMechan titled his appreciation of *Moby-Dick* "The best sea story ever written." He submitted the essay to the major American magazines, all of whom rejected it. He eventually published it in *Queen's Quarterly*, a scholarly Canadian journal. MacMechan's essay ably captures his fondness for *Moby-Dick*. His conclusion reveals how much in tune he was with Melville. His words echo what Ishmael says in "Loomings." MacMechan observed, "Those who feel the salt in their blood that draws them time and again out of the city to the wharves and the ships, almost without their knowledge or their will; those who feel the irresistible lure of the spring, away from the cramped and noisy town, up the long road to the peaceful companionship of the awaking earth and the untainted sky; all those – and there are many – will find in Melville's great book an ever fresh and constant charm" (*Doubloon*, p. 118).

MacMechan promoted Melville as widely as he could. He sent copies of "The best sea story ever written" to influential literary figures in England, Ireland, and North America. One he sent to Samuel Arthur Jones, who thanked him for the essay and told him to send a copy to Henry Salt. MacMechan did what Jones suggested. Thrilled with the essay, Salt reprinted it in the *Humane Review*. An appreciation of an epic whaling hunt may seem an odd inclusion for a magazine largely devoted to animal welfare, but Salt's love of *Moby-Dick* was so unbounded that he made it fit. To MacMechan's essay, he added an extra sentence: "Yet in spite of the savage theme with which it deals, the inner spirit of the book is always a humane one."[8]

After purchasing a copy at a secondhand bookshop in Baltimore while attending graduate school at Johns Hopkins University, MacMechan began sharing *Moby-Dick* with fellow students, including Edward Lucas White, who, in turn, introduced *Moby-Dick* to Frank Jewett Mather, Jr. As Mather recalled, White "haled me to his Baltimore lodging and in the interval of his usual, sonorous recitation of Victor Hugo's and Baudelaire's poetry read me a magnificent seagoing page from *Moby-Dick*. That made me a Melvillian" (*Doubloon*, p. 181). Subsequently, Mather read all the Melville he could get his hands on and what little criticism was available, including Stedman's prefaces and MacMechan's essay. He even imagined writing a biography of Melville.

Humphrey Milford, of the Oxford University Press, considered a new edition of *Moby-Dick* in 1907, but the work would not appear among the Oxford World's Classics until 1920. J. M. Dent issued new editions of *Typee, Omoo*, and *Moby-Dick* in 1907 as part of its Everyman Library. Ernest Rhys, the general editor, called Melville "a writer of sea-tales but a transcendentalist in oilskin, who found a vaster ocean than the Pacific in his own mind, and symbolised in the whale the colossal image of the forces of nature that produce and that overpower man" (*Doubloon*, p. 123). Rhys's respect for Melville is unquestionable. His editorial practice is more circumspect. He based his edition of *Moby-Dick* on the Bentley text. In other words, the Dent edition does not contain the epilogue. Ishmael *still* does not survive. Nicely printed, yet affordable, the Everyman editions brought Melville to many new readers but did not initiate a large-scale revival of interest in Melville.

E. H. Visiak, the Edwardian poet, was one reader who discovered *Moby-Dick* after the Dent edition appeared. He published an appreciative essay in the *New Era* in 1912, recommending "any grim-mouthed ones who cannot get to sea to read *Moby-Dick*, which has salt physic. It is Leviathanic! We are transported to a vast theatre, to tremendous scenes of storm and tragedy upon the sea. The monomaniac Captain Ahab," Visiak continued, "is not the less real because his spirit moves in a Miltonian atmosphere of hell; a demoniac old man, blasted and terrible, with method and policy in his madness, possessing his soul with that frightful patience which makes his every act impressive and grand and condenses every sentence that he utters into drama."[9]

Between Visiak's appreciation and the appearance of the Oxford World's Classics *Moby-Dick*, the world inexorably changed. Before the Great War, Melville's depiction of malevolent nature as symbolized by Moby Dick was too dark for many readers. Surely, evil is not so inherently ingrained in nature as Melville had made it seem. After the war, Melville's viewpoint no longer seemed so far fetched. The darkness, destruction, and undeniable sense of worldly evil brought about by World War I made those qualities in *Moby-Dick* all the more pertinent.

Several new editions of the work appeared during the twenties. The Dent edition became one of the most popular, despite the fact that the numerous reprintings through the 1920s still excluded the epilogue. The exclusion did not seem to matter as much as it had in 1851. E. M. Forster, for example, read *Moby-Dick* in the Dent edition, but the absence of an epilogue scarcely bothered him. He wrote in his commonplace book, "Axiom: Novel must have either one living character or a perfect pattern: fails otherwise. (Though what about Moby Dick?)"[10] What had originally been understood as an unacceptable innovation was now seen as one of the book's unique features.

Other important twentieth-century figures also read *Moby-Dick* in the Dent edition, too. Observing that "Ahab's monomania disturbs and finally destroys all the men on the boat," Jorge Luis Borges implied that he, too, had read *Moby-Dick* in the Dent edition. The great Spanish writer Miguel de Unamuno located a copy of the Dent edition in Paris in 1925 and filled its margins with extensive notes. Thomas Wolfe also read an edition of *Moby-Dick* without the epilogue. John Barrymore, who would play Captain Ahab in *The Sea Beast* (1926), the first film adaptation of the book, read *Moby-Dick* without the epilogue, too. To prepare for his role, Barrymore purchased a copy of the three-volume first edition of *The Whale.*[11]

It is a widely accepted fact that *Moby-Dick* exerted a profound impact on the development of modernism. What has so far escaped notice is that the Bentley text is partly responsible for that impact. This flawed text, this tale told by a dead narrator offered modern authors a challenging new way of storytelling. By the mid twentieth century, the dead narrator would become a storytelling convention. For proof, look no further than *Sunset Boulevard* (1950), in which William Holden's voiceover narration begins as his character, Joe Gillis, floats dead in Norma Desmond's swimming pool.

The most ambitious Melville publishing venture of the 1920s was the sixteen-volume "Standard Edition" prepared by Michael Sadleir and issued by the London firm, Constable and Company. The first six volumes appeared in 1922; the last four, including three volumes of poetry (*Clarel* taking up two of them) and a volume entitled *Billy Budd and Other Prose Pieces*, were released in 1924. (The Constable edition remains the only collected edition of Melville's works ever completed.) Upon the release of this edition, St Loe Strachey observed, "No library, public or private, that professes to represent English literature can possibly be without it."[12] Reviewing the latest volumes, John Middleton Murry contrasted the paucity of Melville's later works with his earlier, prolific output. He observed, "The silence of a great writer needs to be listened to. If he has proved his genius, then his silence is an utterance, and one of no less moment than his speech" (*CR*, p. 549).

The release of the Constable edition let readers discover what other hidden treasures lurked within Melville's oeuvre. What else did Melville write that deserved to be ranked with *Moby-Dick*? With the Melville revival, *Moby-Dick* leaped beyond *Typee* and *Omoo* in the estimate of twentieth-century readers. This is not to say that the earlier books stopped being enjoyed. A new edition of *Omoo*, for example, was published at Boston in 1921; its readers included Robert Frost.[13] Melville's literary style, Frost noticed, has "a certain air of nouveau richness," which he recognized while reading *Typee* aloud (*Doubloon*, p. 247). The Constable edition let readers get to know Melville's lesser known works. Two prominent British litterateurs who acquired the Constable edition recorded their impressions of it for posterity: Arnold Bennett and T. E. Lawrence, that is, Lawrence of Arabia.

Shortly after ordering the complete set, Bennett took delivery of the Constable edition. The sixteen volumes arrived in three large parcels. Upon opening the first two parcels, Bennett realized that *Pierre* remained in the third, unopened parcel. Temporarily, he left it undisturbed. Having heard about *Pierre* from others, he was anxious to read it, but he also wanted to savor the experience and enjoy the anticipation.[14] He did not wait too long. Less than a month after the Constable edition arrived, he had opened the third parcel and devoured *Pierre*. He was not disappointed. He found it "transcendental, even mystical, in spirit," "full of lyrical beauty," and even more daring than the boldest novels of the twentieth century.[15]

Like Bennett, T. E. Lawrence recognized the pertinence of Melville's work to modern times. After obtaining his copy of the Constable edition, Lawrence was torn between his desire to share Melville with others and his reluctance to let any of the individual volumes out of his sight. Hesitantly, he loaned *White-Jacket* to his friend Edward Garnett. Lawrence took the opportunity the Constable edition offered to make new discoveries in Melville. He enjoyed *Pierre* and also liked *Clarel*, which he called one of Melville's finest works. Picture Lawrence of Arabia savoring Melville's poetic journey to the Holy Land. Lawrence's appreciation of *Clarel* is rare: decades would pass before *Clarel* began receiving the attention it deserves. But none of Melville's other books could touch *Moby-Dick*. Lawrence told Garnett that he "collected a shelf of 'Titanic' books (those distinguished by greatness of spirit, 'sublimity' as Longinus would call it)." Besides *Moby-Dick*, Lawrence's shelf of Titanic books included Dostoyevsky's *The brothers Karamazov* and Friedrich Nietzsche's *Thus Spake Zarathustra* (*Doubloon*, p. 149). Distinguished company indeed.

Frank Jewett Mather never did write the Melville biography he planned. That task fell to Raymond Weaver, an English professor at Columbia University. Professor Weaver was not really up to the task. He ignored important biographical sources and slighted Melville's late writings. Despite its faults, Weaver's *Herman Melville, Mariner and Mystic* (1921) will always be the first book-length biography of Melville. The London edition met with a lukewarm reception by those British readers who had been enjoying Melville when their American counterparts were ignoring him. St Loe Strachey began his review as follows: "Anything about Herman Melville and his books is sure to be interesting. But, though this is true, I cannot say that Mr. Weaver's *Herman Melville: Mariner and Mystic* is a great book, or even a satisfactory book. It might so easily be much better and tell us so much more than it does."[16] Like so many of the British litterateurs who contributed to the Melville revival, Strachey had been eagerly anticipating a Melville biography but was disappointed with what Weaver had to say.

John Freeman's *Herman Melville* (1926), was the first book-length work about Melville by an Englishman. Like other volumes in the English Men of Letters series, Freeman's is part biography and part critical appreciation. The biographical part, which draws its detail from Weaver, is outdated, but Freeman's critical appreciation still makes for pleasurable reading. Best remembered as a poet, Freeman writes literary criticism like poetry. His diction is crisp, his syntax impeccable, his ideas heartfelt. Freeman's insightful comments reveal much about Melville's artistry.

Despite its faults, Weaver's biography marks an important shift in the critical reception of Herman Melville. Those who masterminded the Melville revival were English men of letters themselves. With the notable exception of Professor MacMechan, Melvillians of the late nineteenth and early twentieth century were British journalists, novelists, and poets. Once they revived Melville's works, the American academic community took the responsibility of doing the kind of hard-nosed, biographical, historical, bibliographical, and textual scholarship that every great writer deserves. In the mid-twenties, the Melville revival gave way to the Melville industry.

Numerous editions of Melville's works appeared through the late 1920s and into the 1930s. The revival spread to other countries, too. *Typee* appeared in French (1926), German (1927), Russian (1929), and Italian (1932). Translations of *Moby-Dick* appeared in Finnish (1928), French (1928), German (1929), and Italian (1932). Translations of other works during the 1930s show France's burgeoning interest in Melville. A French version of *Benito Cereno* appeared in 1937. Two years later "The Lightning-Rod Man" was translated into French and published as a separate pamphlet. A French translation of *Pierre* appeared in 1939 and so did a new translation of *Moby-Dick*. That same year, the first book-length critical study in French appeared, Jean Simon's *Herman Melville: marin, métaphysicien, et poète*.

The experience of Jean Giono, the novelist who co-translated *Moby-Dick* in the 1930s, captures the French enthusiasm for Melville. Giono recalled, "This book was my foreign companion. I'd always take it to my wanderings across the hills. So at the very moment when I often perused these great solitudes immobile yet undulating like the ocean, all I needed to do was to sit down my back against the trunk of a pine tree, and take out that book already lapping to feel underneath and around me the swelling of many lives of the ocean." These words introduce *Pour saluer Melville* (1941), a fictional work that pays tribute to Melville's life and writings.

Important scholarly studies began appearing, too. The most renowned book on Melville to emerge during the 1920s is Lewis Mumford's *Herman Melville* (1929). A fine writer himself, Mumford sometimes let his literary skills get the better of his judgement. His text frequently shades into fiction without giving readers fair warning. The two most important studies of Melville to emerge during the 1930s are Willard Thorp's *Herman Melville: Representative Selections* (1938) and C. R. Anderson's *Melville in the South Seas* (1939). Thorp's work, an anthology intended for classroom use, includes an exemplary 150-page introduction. Based on original research and written with style and sense, Thorp's introduction ranks among the best appreciations of Melville. For his book, Anderson searched through many contemporary newspapers, books, and archives to put the years Melville spent as a sailor into context. Both works embody a level of seriousness and dedication that would become hallmarks of the best Melville scholarship in the decades to come.

Many critical studies appeared during the 1940s, most in the form of articles written for popular magazines and scholarly journals. By 1948, Melville criticism had proliferated to such an extent that Jack Kerouac proclaimed, "Today critics cream all over *Moby Dick*."[17] Despite the lack of subtlety, Kerouac's words show how Melville's critical reception had changed. Gone were the days when Fleet Street buzzed with talk of Melville after the appearance of the Oxford World's Classics edition of *Moby-Dick*. Melville had entered the mainstream.

During the late 1940s, *Moby-Dick* became a classroom standard. Professors across the United States and around the world were regularly assigning the book to their students and sharing with them a very special reading experience. Given its ubiquity in the college classroom, *Moby-Dick* accumulated a layer of chalk dust it found difficult to shake off. Readers began longing for a fresh approach, a way to experience Melville outside the academy, a way to make it seem as if they were discovering him for the first time. *The Confidence-Man* offered such an opportunity.

Though Michael Sadleir had included *The Confidence-Man* in the Constable edition, it had had little impact in the 1920s. Few readers of the time even mentioned it. Neither Arnold Bennett nor T. E. Lawrence said anything about the book in their published comments. Freeman called it "considerable in bulk, negligible in quality." *Romances of Herman Melville*, a fat one-volume collected edition of Melville's book-length works published in 1928, omitted both *Pierre* and *The Confidence-Man*. The publishers explained in the preface that *The Confidence-Man* deserved a "place beside *Pierre* as a book that does not transmit to us its author's greatness."[18] But in the late 1940s, *The Confidence-Man* emerged as a major work in Melville's oeuvre, second only to *Moby-Dick* in importance.

James Laughlin, the publisher of New Directions, considered reissuing a new edition of *The Confidence-Man* in the mid-1940s but decided that the time was not right.[19] In 1948, John Lehmann did republish *The Confidence-Man* in London as part of the prestigious Chiltern Library. In his introduction to this edition, Roy Fuller identified the inexplicitness of its plot as a prominent feature of the book. Melville's inexplicitness, Fuller argued, was less like Robert Louis Stevenson's and more like Kafka's. *The Confidence-Man* shared another affinity to Kafka's work. Despite the ingenuity of the plot, "there is hardly any attempt to exploit it for the sake of entertainment or neatness."[20] The work's modernity made it an ideal work for readers seeking a Melville unencumbered by the stodginess imposed by the term "literary classic." The reception history of *The Confidence-Man* shows how the study of Melville was revitalized even after he earned the reputation of a great American writer.

Jack Kerouac got caught up in the growing enthusiasm for *The Confidence-Man*, too. His reference to the book occurs in a 1950 letter to his friend Neal Cassady in which he explains how he was struggling to find his own unique literary voice. Kerouac observed, "Melville in *Confidence Man* is the strangest voice ever heard in America." After studying Melville's narrative technique in *The Confidence-Man* and in such shorter works as "Benito Cereno" and "Billy Budd," Kerouac was able to develop his own unique narrative style. The letter to Cassady reveals another aspect of how Kerouac read *The Confidence-Man*: he said there was no better book to read while high.[21]

Kerouac did not say which edition of *The Confidence-Man* he read, but it almost surely was the Grove Press edition, which first appeared the year before his letter to Cassady. Issued in a small-format, paperback edition, the Grove *Confidence-Man* presents a series of excerpts from Melville criticism on its back cover headed "92 years of *The Confidence-Man*." The excerpts include a quotation from the review by George Meredith (unattributed); Lewis Mumford's epithet for *The Confidence-Man*: "a companion volume to *Gulliver's Travels*"; and Richard Chase's statement that the book was Melville's "second-best achievement." The oddest remark in this list is the one by the "uncircumspect critic" quoted from Weaver's biography: "His last few books, such as *Pierre* and *The Confidence-Man* are quite incomprehensible." Earlier reviewers critiqued the book's incomprehensibility; in the mid twentieth century, that incomprehensibility became one of the book's selling points. The publisher's introduction to the first printing of the Grove *Confidence-Man* vividly describes Melville's growing importance to literary history: "Slowly, like a mountain emerging from a late morning fog, the stature of Melville is being discerned."[22]

The importance of this edition has so far gone unnoticed. Over the next decade, Grove Press would develop a reputation as a daring, innovative

publisher responsible for bringing to American readers some of the most challenging contemporary literature available. Samuel Beckett, Jean Genet, Eugene
Ionesco, Alain Robbe-Grillet: all reached American readers in editions published by Grove Press. But the press's very first imprint was *The Confidence-Man*.
Herman Melville launched Grove Press.

Of course, Barney Rosset, who took control of Grove Press in the early
1950s, deserves credit for putting the press in the publishing vanguard. But
even as Rosset was recruiting important new twentieth-century authors, he
was expanding his Melville list. He kept *The Confidence-Man* in print, rereleas-
ing it in the popular "Evergreen Books" series in 1955. Grove released a new
edition of *White-Jacket* in 1956 and a new edition of *Pierre* in 1957. Grove also
issued multiple works of Melville criticism outside mainstream academic criticism, including a reprint of Charles Olson's idiosyncratic *Call Me Ishmael*; John
Ashbery's translation of Jean-Jacques Mayoux's *Melville*; and A. R. Humphrey's
Herman Melville. Published alongside Beckett and Genet, the primary and sec-
ondary Melville works Grove published offered readers what could be termed
Alternative Melville.

French readers shared much the same experience. *Le grand escroc*, as the
French translation of *The Confidence-Man* was entitled, became a symbol of
the avant-garde after its initial publication in 1950. Jean-Luc Godard borrowed
the French title of Melville's novel for his short film, *Le grand escroc* (1963). The
film is not an adaptation per se, but it was inspired by Melville and pays homage
to the book. Jean Seberg, who appears reading a copy of Melville's novel, plays
a documentary filmmaker named Patricia Leacock. The name of her character
refers to the pioneer of *cinéma vérité*, Richard Leacock. Godard's basic point is
that any filmmaker who practiced *cinéma vérité* is a kind of confidence man.
Both *Le grand escroc* and *The Confidence-Man* exemplify what Gilles Deleuze
called the power of the false.[23] Godard's playful film confirms that Melville's
ideas pertain to forms of expression unknown in his day.

Ultimately, *The Confidence-Man* underwent an experience similar to what
happened to *Moby-Dick*. Inexpensive classroom editions appeared in the
late sixties and early seventies, and the book started being widely taught.
English professors began writing scholarly monographs devoted solely to *The
Confidence-Man*. As the work gained the status of a literary classic, it took on
the weighty cultural baggage that comes with that label and lost some of the
mystique that had made it such an exciting book to read in the 1950s.

Though the reputation of *The Confidence-Man* has waned in recent decades,
other works let readers approach Melville in fresh new ways. *Pierre* has leapt
over *The Confidence-Man* in terms of literary importance. What was once said
about *The Confidence-Man* is now being said about *Pierre*: it is Melville's best

work after *Moby-Dick*. In the not-too-distant future, the reputation of *Pierre* may wane, and another may take its place. Melville remarked that time would eventually solve the riddle of *Mardi*. Or perhaps *Clarel* will emerge to take the place of *Pierre* as Melville's second-best work. Regardless how his books sort themselves out in terms of relative importance, one thing seems certain: The works of Herman Melville will continue to offer readers many new and exciting opportunities for discovery.

Notes

1 Life

1. [Christian Isobel Johnston,] "Literary Register," *Tait's Edinburgh Magazine*, 13 (1846), 268; Parke Godwin, "Letters from America," *People's Journal*, 4 (14 August 1847), 84.
2. "St. Louis Statistics," *Western Journal of Agriculture, Manufactures, Mechanic Arts, Internal Improvements, Commerce, and General Literature*, 2 (1849), 209; "Ship News," *Times*, 2 October 1850, 7; "Ship News," *Times*, 15 July 1852, 8; "Sporting Intelligence," *Times*, 18 October 1861, 7; "The Bombay and Mauritius Mails," *Times*, 15 July 1864, 9.
3. Lydia Maria Child, "The Hindoo Anchorite," *Union Magazine of Literature and Art*, 2 (1848), 151; Seth Pancoast, *The Ladies Medical Guide*, 6th edn. (Philadelphia: John E. Potter, 1865), 543; Mary Hughs, *May Morning: or A Visit to the Country, for Little Boys and Little Girls* (Philadelphia: Lindsay and Blakiston, 1849), 55, notes, "This account is chiefly taken from a work entitled *Narrative of a Four Months' Residence in the Marquesas. By Herman Melville.*"
4. [T. K. Hervey,] "*The Story of Toby*: a sequel to *Typee*," *Athenaeum*, 988 (3 October 1846), 1014–1015.
5. [Robert Bell,] "Literature of the Month," *Bentley's Miscellany*, 26 (1849), 528–530; Ibid., 27 (1850), 309–310.
6. Jean-Jacques Mayoux, *Melville*, translated by John Ashbery (New York: Grove Press, 1960), 111.
7. Henry James, "American Letter," *Literature*, 2 (1899), 676–677.

2 Contexts

1. Merton M. Sealts, Jr, "Melville," in *American Literary Scholarship: An Annual, 1967*, edited by James Woodress (Durham: Duke University Press, 1969), 32.
2. Henri Lefebvre, *Writings on Cities*, translated by Eleonore Kofman and Elizabeth Lebas (Oxford: Blackwell, 1996), 226–230.
3. Donald Phelps, "The Holy Family," *Prose*, 5 (1972), 106.

4. Walter Benjamin, *The Arcades Project*, translated by Howard Eiland and Kevin McLaughlin, edited by Rolf Tiedemann (Cambridge, MA: The Belknap Press of Harvard University Press, 1999), 419.

5. Eric Rohmer, *The Taste for Beauty*, translated by Carol Volk (New York: Cambridge University Press, 1989), 107.

6. Henry Nash Smith, "The Madness of Ahab," in *The Critical Response to Herman Melville's Moby-Dick*, edited by Kevin J. Hayes (Westport, CT: Greenwood Press, 1994), 183–200.

7. Edwin Fussell, "*Moby-Dick* and the American West," in Hayes (ed.), *Critical Response*, 99–117.

8. Charles Olson, *Collected Prose*, edited by Donald Allen and Benjamin Friedlander (Berkeley: University of California Press, 1997), 18.

9. Walker Cowen, *Melville's Marginalia*, 2 vols. (New York: Garland, 1987), I, 649.

10. Charles Burchfield, "A Magnificent Feeling," in Hayes (ed.), *Critical Response*, 61; C. L. R. James, *Mariners, Renegades and Castaways: The Story of Herman Melville and the World We Live In* (Hanover: University Press of New England, 2001), 28.

11. Mukhtar Ali Isani, "Melville and the 'Bloody Battle in Affghanistan," *American Quarterly*, 20 (1968), 645–649.

3 Writings

1. Lewis Mumford, *Herman Melville* (New York: Harcourt Brace and Co. 1929), 82.

2. John Freeman, *Herman Melville* (New York: Macmillan, 1926), 166.

3. Frederick Douglass, *My Bondage and My Freedom* (New York: Miller, Orton, 1857), 142.

4. John Milton, *Paradise Lost*, in *Complete Poems and Major Prose*, edited by Merritt Y. Hughes (New York: Macmillan, 1957), book 3, line 44; Alexander Pope (trans.), *The Iliad of Homer* (London: Bernard Lintot, 1720), book 23, line 506; William Julius Mickle (trans.), *The Lusiad; or, The Discovery of India* (Oxford: Jackson and Lister, 1776), 302.

5. T. Walter Herbert, Jr, *Marquesans Encounters: Melville and the Meaning of Civilization* (Cambridge, MA: Harvard University Press, 1980), 158.

6. Charles Olson quoted in Clare L. Spark, *Hunting Captain Ahab: Psychological Warfare and the Melville Revival* (Kent, OH: Kent State University Press, 2001), p. 288.

7. Walter Benjamin, *The Arcades Project*, translated by Howard Eiland and Kevin McLaughlin, edited by Rolf Tiedemann (Cambridge, MA: Belknap Press of Harvard University Press, 1999), 418.

8. [J. A. Heraud,] review of *Omoo*, *Athenaeum*, 1015 (10 April 1847), 382–384; Charles Richard Sanders, et al. (eds.), *The Collected Letters of Thomas and Jane Welsh Carlyle*

(Durham, NC: Duke University Press, 1970–), XII, 92; Sergei Eisenstein, *Beyond the Stars: The Memoirs of Sergei Eisenstein*, translated by William Powell, edited by Richard Taylor (London: BFI, 1995), 358.

9. Robert Sattelmeyer, "Thoreau and Melville's *Typee*," *American Literature*, 52 (1980), 464.

10. John St Loe Strachey, "The Complete Works of Herman Melville," *Spectator*, 26 May 1923, 887.

11. Walker Cowen, *Melville's Marginalia*, 2 vols. (New York: Garland, 1987), I, 513.

12. "Item Details: *Omoo*," 2004, *Heritage Book Shop, Inc.*, 2 April 2005, www.heritagebookshop.com, describes a copy of the 1847 London edition with Edward Lear's signature dated 1856 on the title page.

13. Willard Thorp (ed.), *Herman Melville: Representative Selections* (New York: American Book Company, 1938), lxv.

14. John Evelev, "'Every One to His Trade': *Mardi*, literary form, and professional ideology," *American Literature*, 75 (2003), 305–333.

15. Brian Foley, "Herman Melville and the Example of Sir Thomas Browne," in *The Critical Response to Herman Melville's Moby-Dick*, edited by Kevin J. Hayes (Westport, CT: Greenwood Press, 1994), 201–220.

16. Newton Arvin, *Herman Melville* (New York: William Sloane, 1950), 105.

17. Kevin J. Hayes, *Melville's Folk Roots* (Kent, Ohio: Kent State University Press, 1999), 29.

18. Peter Brunette (ed.), *Martin Scorsese: Interviews* (Jackson: University Press of Mississippi, 1999), 96–97.

19. Freeman, *Herman Melville*, 60.

20. Quoted in Hershel Parker, *Herman Melville: A Biography*, 2 vols. (Baltimore: Johns Hopkins University Press, 1996–2002), II, 47.

21. Jean-Jacques Mayoux, *Melville*, translated by John Ashbery (New York: Grove Press, 1960), 69.

22. Parker, *Herman Melville*, I, 816.

23. Roland Barthes, *Camera Lucida: Reflections on Photography*, translated by Richard Howard (New York: Hill and Wang, 1981), 98.

24. Edward J. O'Brien, "The Fifteen Finest Short Stories," *Forum*, 79 (1928), 909.

25. Robert Emmet Long (ed.), *John Huston: Interviews* (Jackson: University Press of Mississippi, 2001), 14.

26. A. R. Humphreys, *Herman Melville* (New York: Grove Press, 1962), 99.

27. Hershel Parker, "Melville's Salesman's Story," *Studies in Short Fiction*, 1 (1963), 154–158.

28. Q. D. Leavis, "Melville: the 1853–6 phase," in Faith Pullin (ed.), *New Perspectives on Melville* (Edinburgh: Edinburgh University Press, 1978), 208.

29. Kennth D. Pimple, "Personal Narrative, Melville's *The Confidence-Man*, and the Problem of Deception," *Western Folklore*, 51 (1992), 36.

30. J. A. Leo Lemay, "The Text, Tradition, and Themes of 'The Big Bear of Arkansas,'" *American Literature*, 47 (1975), 321–342.

31. Kevin J. Hayes, "Melville and Balzac," *Resources for American Literary Study*, 26 (2000), 164–166.

32. C. L. R. James, *Mariners, Renegades and Castaways: The Story of Herman Melville and the World We Live In* (Hanover: University Press of New England, 2001), 107.

33. Kent Ljungquist, "'Meteor of the War': Melville, Thoreau, and Whitman Respond to John Brown," *American Literature*, 61 (1989), 674–680.

34. J. Watts De Peyster, *Personal and Military History of Philip Kearny* (New York: Rice and Gage, 1869), 474–475.

35. Cowen, *Melville's Marginalia*, II, 192.

36. Cowen, *Melville's Marginalia*, II, 193.

37. "New Books," *Ohio Farmer*, 15 (15 September 1866), 291.

38. Stanton Garner, *The Civil War World of Herman Melville* (Lawrence: University Press of Kansas, 1993), 139.

39. Hennig Cohen (ed.), *The Battle-Pieces of Herman Melville* (New York: Thomas Yoseloff, 1964), 219.

40. "Editorial Notes, etc.," *Debow's Review*, 2 (1866), 557.

41. Cohen (ed.), *Battle-Pieces*, 295.

42. Patrick J. White, *Berryman's Dream Songs and the American Long Verse Epic Tradition* (Newark: University of Delaware, 1993).

43. Richard Chase, *Herman Melville: A Critical Study* (New York: Macmillan, 1949), 242.

44. White, *Berryman's Dream Songs*, 58.

45. [John Richard de Capel Wise,] "Belles Lettres," *Westminster Review*, 105 (1876), 577–578.

46. Arvin, *Herman Melville*, 273.

47. Padraic Colum, "Moby Dick as an Epic: A Note," *The Measure: A Journal of Poetry*, 13 (March 1922), 16–18.

48. Quoted in André Breton, *Manifestoes of Surrealism*, translated by Richard Seaver and Helen R. Lane (Ann Arbor: University of Michigan Press, 1969), 20.

49. Hayes, *Melville's Folk Roots*, 96–97.

50. White, *Berryman's Dream Songs*, 171–172.

51. Hayes, *Melville's Folk Roots*, 88–89.

52. Robert A. Sandberg (ed.), "'House of the Tragic Poet': Melville's draft of a preface to his unfinished Burgundy Club book," *Melville Society Extracts*, 79 (November 1989), 5.

53. Freeman, *Herman Melville*, 164.

54. Sandberg (ed.), "'House of the Tragic Poet,'" 5.

55. Junius Henri Browne, *The Great Metropolis: A Mirror of New York* (Hartford: American Publishing, 1869), p. 446.

56. Cowen, *Melville's Marginalia*, I, 511.

57. Hayes, "Melville and Balzac," 180.

58. Humphreys, *Herman Melville*, 113.

59. Hershel Parker, *Reading Billy Budd* (Evanston: Northwestern University Press, 1990), 115, 119.
60. John Wenke, "Melville's Indirection: *Billy Budd*, the Genetic Text, and 'The Deadly Space Between,'" in *New Essays on Billy Budd*, edited by Donald Yannella (New York: Cambridge University Press, 2002), 126.
61. C. N. Manlove, "An Organic Hesitancy: Theme and Style in *Billy Budd*," in Pullin (ed.), *New perspectives on Melville*, 281.
62. John Wenke, "Complicating Vere: Melville's Practice of Revision in *Billy Budd*," *Leviathan*, 1 (1999), 85.

4 Reception

1. Sidney Colvin (ed.), *The Letters of Robert Louis Stevenson*, 2 vols. (London: Methuen, 1899), II, 115; Robert Louis Stevenson, "The South Seas: A Record of Three Cruises," *Black and White*, 1 (1891), 114; Robert Louis Stevenson and Lloyd Osbourne, *The Wrecker* (1892; reprinted, New York: Oxford University Press, 1954), 134.
2. "New publications," *Cultivator*, 9 (1852), 320.
3. [Henry Fothergill Chorley,] review of *Israel Potter*, *Athenaeum*, 2 June 1855, 643.
4. [George Meredith,] "Belles Lettres and Art," *Westminster and Foreign Quarterly Review*, 12 (1857), 310–311.
5. *Massachusetts Teacher and Journal of Home and School Education*, 19 (October 1866), 362.
6. Frederick J. Kennedy, "Dr. Samuel Arthur Jones and Herman Melville," *Melville Society Extracts*, 32 (1977), 4.
7. Theodore Dreiser's annotated copy of *Typee* survives at the University of Pennsylvania.
8. Frederick James Kennedy and Joyce Deveau Kennedy, "Archibald MacMechan and the Melville Revival," *Leviathan*, 1 (1999), 5–37.
9. E. H. Visiak, "Moby Dick," *New Age*, 25 January 1912, 304–205.
10. E. M. Forster, *Commonplace Book*, edited by Philip Gardner (Stanford: Stanford University Press, 1985), 6.
11. Jorge Luis Borges, "Prologue to Herman Melville's 'Bartleby,'" *in Herman Melville's Billy Budd, "Benito Cereno," "Bartleby, the scrivener," and Other Tales*, edited by Harold Bloom (New York: Chelsea House, 1987), 8; Thomas Wolfe's annotated copy of *Moby-Dick* survives at Harvard University; Manuel Garcia Blanco, "Unamuno y el novelista norteamericano Melville," *Insula*, 19 (1964), 216–217; for Barrymore's copy of *The Whale*, see *The Maurice F. Neville Collection of Modern Literature* (New York: Sotheby's, 2004), lot 174.
12. John St Loe Strachey, "The Complete Works of Herman Melville," *Spectator*, 26 May 1923, 887.
13. Robert Frost's copy of *Omoo* survives at the University of Virginia.

14. Arnold Bennett, *The Journal of Arnold Bennett* (New York: The Literary Guild, 1933), 877.

15. Andrew Mylett (ed.), *Arnold Bennett: The Evening Standard Years, "Books and Persons," 1926–1931* (London: Chatto and Windus, 1974), 13.

16. John St Loe Strachey, "Herman Melville: Mariner and Mystic," *Spectator*, 6 May, 1922, 559–560.

17. Jack Kerouac, *Selected Letters, 1940–1956*, edited by Ann Charters (New York: Viking, 1995), 173.

18. John Freeman, *Herman Melville* (New York: Macmillan, 1926), 62; "Preface," *Romances of Herman Melville* (New York: Pickwick Publishers, 1928), vi.

19. Clare L. Spark, *Hunting Captain Ahab: Psychological Warfare and the Melville Revival* (Kent, OH: Kent State University Press, 2001), 483.

20. Roy Fuller, "Introduction," in *The Confidence-Man: His Masquerade*, edited by Elizabeth S. Foster (London: John Lehmann, 1948), viii–ix.

21. *Fine Books and Manuscripts Including Americana: New York, Wednesday, December 10, 2003* (New York: Sotheby's, 2003), lot 127, lists Kerouac's inscribed copy of *The Shorter Novels of Herman Melville* (1942); Kerouac, *Selected Letters*, 233.

22. Elizabeth S. Foster (ed.), "A Note on the Author," *The Confidence-Man: His Masquerade* (New York: Grove Press, 1949), iv.

23. Gilles Deleuze, *Cinema 2: The Time-Image*, translated by Hugh Tomlinson and Robert Galeta (Minneapolis: University of Minnesota Press, 1989), 132–133.

Guide to further reading

Exemplary editions

Foster, Elizabeth S. (ed.), *The Confidence-Man: His Masquerade*, New York: Hendricks House, 1954. Published soon after *The Confidence-Man* revival, Foster's meticulous edition illuminates some of the novel's complexities. Her lengthy introduction situates the book within its cultural milieu; her extensive notes explain the novel's arcane historical and contemporary references.

Hayford, Harrison, and Walter Blair (eds.), *Omoo: A Narrative of Adventures in the South Seas*, New York: Hendricks House, 1969. Though publication of this edition was delayed for several years, it has withstood the test of time. Hayford's unsurpassed annotations reveal the richness of images and ideas that fill *Omoo*, Melville's most undervalued work.

Hayford, Harrison, and Merton M. Sealts, Jr (eds.), *Billy Budd, Sailor (An Inside Narrative): Reading Text and Genetic Text*, Chicago: University of Chicago Press, 1962. This, the standard edition of Melville's last novel, presents both the reading text of *Billy Budd* and the genetic text, which transcribes Melville's manuscript, identifying the different stages and substages of composition.

Hayford, Harrison, G. Thomas Tanselle, and Hershel Parker (eds.), *The Writings of Herman Melville*, 13 vols. to date, Evanston and Chicago: Northwestern University Press and The Newberry Library, 1968– (vols. 1–10, 12, 14–15). Each volume in this edition contains a detailed historical essay placing the work in its biographical, historical, and critical contexts. The editorial policy for the early volumes omitted explanatory notes, but during its lengthy publication, the policy has changed. Some of the more recent volumes in this collected edition – *Journals, Clarel* – include excellent annotations.

Mansfield, Luther S., and Howard P. Vincent (eds.), *Moby-Dick: or, The Whale*, New York: Hendricks House, 1952. The splendidly annotated Mansfield-Vincent text of *Moby-Dick* is essential for understanding the literary, historical, and cultural references that contribute so much to the work's richness.

Parker, Hershel (ed.), and Maurice Sendak (illus.), *Pierre: or, The Ambiguities*, New York: HarperCollins, 1995. This edition approximates the text of *Pierre* as it stood once Melville first completed the work in late 1851, that is, before

130

the negative reviews of *Moby-Dick* appeared and Melville expanded his text and turned Pierre Glendinning into an author. Sendak's provocative illustrations constitute a challenging, yet sensitive interpretation of the novel in themselves.

Sanborn, Geoffrey (ed.), *Typee: Complete Text with Introduction, Historical Contexts, Critical Essays*, Boston: Houghton Mifflin, 2004. This edition not only presents a reading text of *Typee*, it also includes numerous supporting documents. The accounts from contemporary explorers of the South Seas treat many of the same themes as Melville and thus serve as vital touchstones for *Typee*.

Biography

Garner, Stanton, *The Civil War World of Herman Melville*, Lawrence: University Press of Kansas, 1993. The single best treatment of *Battle-Pieces*, this work presents a detailed history of each of the events that inspired Melville's collection of Civil War verse. Essentially a critical biography of Melville during the Civil War years, this work has one drawback: a tendency to devote too much space to Melville's extended family, a tendency that plagues even the best Melville biographies.

Heflin, Wilson L., *Herman Melville's Whaling Years*, Nashville: Vanderbilt University Press, 2004. A collection of articles Heflin published throughout his career, this volume offers much important information for reassessing Melville's life as a sailor before he turned author.

Leyda, Jay, *The Melville Log: A Documentary Life of Herman Melville, 1819–1891*, 1951; reprinted, New York: Gordian Press, 1969. A carefully-crafted compilation of source materials excerpted from contemporary documents – journals, letters, newspaper accounts, reviews – and assembled according to Sergei Eisenstein's principles of montage, *The Melville Log* is the single most important work of Melville scholarship ever created.

Parker, Hershel, *Herman Melville: A Biography*, 2 vols., Baltimore: Johns Hopkins University Press, 1996–2002. Two-thousand pages in length, Parker's is the most thorough biography of Melville available and contains much new information. More than merely a literary biography of an individual author, this work constitutes a grand saga of the Melville family.

Reference works

Bercaw, Mary K. *Melville's Sources*, Evanston: Northwestern University Press, 1987. The second part of this innovative bibliography lists scholarly books and articles identifying literary sources that influenced Melville. Drawing its information from these scholarly works, the first part offers a bibliography of sources. Bercaw's work is essential for understanding the literary contexts of Melville's writings.

Cowen, Walker, *Melville's Marginalia*, 2 vols., New York: Garland, 1987. Cowen transcribes the holograph inscriptions – both verbal and non-verbal – from surviving copies of books formerly in Melville's possession. *Melville's Marginalia* offers an excellent way to see how Melville read what he read.

Hayes, Kevin J., and Hershel Parker, *Checklist of Melville Reviews*, Evanston: Northwestern University Press, 1991. Designed as a research tool, this checklist is slim enough to be tucked into a briefcase and toted to the library for ready reference while scanning through old newspapers on microfilm. While containing the fullest listing of contemporary reviews available, this checklist is intended as a work in progress. Many more reviews await discovery.

Higgins, Brian, *Herman Melville, An Annotated Bibliography*, Boston: G. K. Hall, 1979. Higgins lists articles and books about Melville from 1846, the year *Typee* appeared, to 1930. His annotations show his keen understanding of Melville criticism. Taken together, these entries offer an overview of Melville's contemporary reception, subsequent neglect, and ultimate revival.

Higgins, Brian, *Herman Melville: A Reference Guide, 1931–1960*, Boston: G. K. Hall, 1987. Picking up where Higgins's earlier bibliography left off, this work traces Melville scholarship and criticism from the period of the 1930s and 1940s – the golden age of literary scholarship – through the heyday of the New Criticism to the beginnings of post-structural criticism.

Sealts, Merton M., Jr, *Melville's Reading: Revised and Enlarged Edition*, Columbia: University of South Carolina Press, 1988. Sealts's thorough introduction shows how important books were to Melville's life. The bulk of this work presents a catalogue of books Melville owned or read. Brief annotations to the individual bibliographic entries describe the evidence underlying Sealts's identifications.

Retrospective essay collections

Hayes, Kevin (ed.), *The Critical Response to Herman Melville's Moby-Dick*, Westport, CT: Greenwood Press, 1994. Subdivided into three sections, this collection surveys the critical reception of *Moby-Dick* from the contemporary response through the Melville revival to modern academic attention. Largely filled with reprinted articles, this collection includes two original essays, the editor's "*Moby-Dick* and the Aesthetics of Response" and Mark Niemeyer's "*Moby-Dick* and the Spirit of Revolution."

Higgins, Brian, and Hershel Parker (eds.), *Critical Essays on Herman Melville's Moby-Dick*, New York: G. K. Hall, 1992. This beefy work includes a good selection of contemporary reviews, critical articles, essays treating the literary influences on and major themes of *Moby-Dick*, and original essays by John Wenke, David S. Reynolds, and Hershel Parker.

Higgins, Brian, and Hershel Parker (eds.), *Herman Melville: The Contemporary Reviews*, New York: Cambridge University Press, 1995. The fullest collection of Melville reviews available, this invaluable collection contains a wealth of useful information for understanding Melville's contemporary reception. The only drawback – a poor index – can be mitigated by consulting the electronic edition, which is available online.

Parker, Hershel and Harrison Hayford (eds.), *Moby-Dick as Doubloon: Essays and Extracts (1851–1970)*, New York: W. W. Norton, 1970. Since most of the included works are extracts rather than complete essays, this collection makes for a fast-paced survey of some of the most insightful comments by some of the best writers who have commented on Melville's masterwork.

Critical studies

Arvin, Newton, *Herman Melville*, 1950; reprinted, New York: Grove, 2002. Often mislabeled a biography, Arvin's critical study contains many incisive comments on Melville's life and work. Paradoxically, Arvin's greatest strength is also his greatest weakness. He interprets Melville's life as his own. Sometimes Arvin is on target; other times he lets his own personal orientation color his understanding of Melville's life.

Bryant, John, *Melville and Repose: The Rhetoric of Humor in the American Renaissance*, New York: Oxford University Press, 1993. Bryant initially situates Melville within the comic tradition in American literature, examining Washington Irving, Edgar Allan Poe, and Thomas Bangs Thorpe as Melville's literary forebears. After providing this foundation, Bryant discusses Melville's use of humor in *Typee*, *Moby-Dick*, and *The Confidence-Man* at length.

Bryant, John, and Robert Milder (eds.), *Melville's Evermoving Dawn: Centennial Essays*, Kent, OH: Kent State University Press, 1997. This eclectic collection contains essays by some of the most important Melville scholars available: Walter Bezanson, H. Bruce Franklin, Stanton Garner, Hershel Parker, Merton Sealts, John Seelye, and many others. The highlight of the collection is a transcript of a panel discussion on Melville biography.

Grey, Robin (ed.), *Melville and Milton: An Edition and Analysis of Melville's Annotations on Milton*, Pittsburgh: Duquesne University Press, 2004. In addition to transcribing Melville's marginalia from his copy of Milton, Grey includes critical essays by several contributors analyzing Milton's influence on *Battle-Pieces*, *Clarel*, and *Moby-Dick*.

Hayes, Kevin J., *Melville's Folk Roots*, Kent, Ohio: Kent State University Press, 1999. The first part of this work contains five chapters, each devoted to a different folk genre: folk songs, legends, proverbs, superstitions, and tall tales. The chapters that form the second part examine individual works that make significant use of folklore: *Clarel*, *Moby-Dick*, and *Redburn*.

Hayford, Harrison, *Melville's Prisoners*, Evanston: Northwestern University Press, 2003. A compilation of essays published throughout Hayford's career, this volume is filled with valuable insights into Melville's life and writings. Especially important are Hayford's discussions of Melville's compositional process.

James, C. L. R., *Mariners, Renegades, and Castaways: The Story of Herman Melville and the World We Live In*, 1953; reprinted, Hanover: University Press of New England, 2001. The fullest and finest reading of Melville from a Marxist point of view, *Mariners, Renegades, and Castaways* identifies Melville's affinity to twentieth-century sociopolitical developments and provides detailed critical interpretations of *Moby-Dick* and *Pierre*.

Olson, Charles, *Collected Prose*, Donald Allen and Benjamin Friedlander, eds., Berkeley: University of California Press, 1997. *Call Me Ishmael*, Olson's classic study of Melville's writing, remains an intriguing work, even if it is a little fast and loose in the fact department. This collection also includes three review-essays that discuss new editions and critical studies of Melville.

Parker, Hershel, *Reading Billy Budd*, Evanston: Northwestern University Press, 1990. This, the fullest critical treatment of *Billy Budd*, puts the work in the context of Melville's late writings, examines its textual history, provides a detailed chapter-by-chapter analysis, and identifies the problematical nature of the text.

Robillard, Douglas, *Melville and the Visual Arts: Ionian Form, Venetian Tint*, Kent, OH: Kent State University Press, 1997. In his early chapters, Robillard describes what Melville knew about art from his reading, his gallery visits, and his collection of engravings. Individual chapters analyze the place of art in *Clarel, Moby-Dick, Pierre*, and *Redburn*.

Wenke, John P., *Melville's Muse: Literary Creation and the Forms of Philosophical Fiction*, Kent, Ohio: Kent State University Press, 1995. Analyzing the place of philosophy in Melville's fiction, Wenke begins with an extensive treatment of *Mardi*, offers multiple perspectives on *Moby-Dick*, and closes with discussions of *Pierre* and *The Confidence-Man*.

Index